MW00445315

When Suffering
Is Redemptive

For Cliff,
Whose care, generosity,
love, availability, & in-
vestment in me almost
fifty years ago has been my
model for how I should treat
others ever since.

Gratefully,
Mark
8 September 2017

When Suffering Is Redemptive

Stories of How
Anguish and Pain
Accomplish God's Mission

Edited by **LARRY J. WATERS**
Foreword by **JONI EARECKSON TADA**

WEAVER BOOK
COMPANY
WOOSTER, OHIO

When Suffering Is Redemptive: Stories of How Anguish and Pain Accomplish God's Mission
© 2016 by Larry J. Waters

Published by Weaver Book Company, 1190 Summerset Dr., Wooster, OH 44691
weaverbookcompany.com

All rights reserved. No part of this book may be reproduced, stored in a retrieval system, or transmitted in any form or by any means—electronic, mechanical, photocopy, recording or otherwise—without written permission of the publisher, except for brief quotations in printed reviews.

Scripture quotations marked ESV are from The Holy Bible, English Standard Version® (ESV®), copyright © 2001 by Crossway, a publishing ministry of Good News Publishers. Used by permission. All rights reserved.

Scripture quotations marked NASB are from the New American Standard Bible®. Copyright © 1960, 1962, 1963, 1968, 1971, 1972, 1973, 1975, 1977, 1995 by The Lockman Foundation. Used by permission. www.Lockman.org.

Scripture quotations marked NIV are from the Holy Bible, New International Version®, NIV®. Copyright © 1973, 1978, 1984, 2011 by Biblica, Inc.™ Used by permission of Zondervan. All rights reserved worldwide. www.zondervan.com.

Scripture quotations marked NKJV are from the New King James Version®. Copyright © 1982 by Thomas Nelson, Inc. Used by permission. All rights reserved.

Scripture quotations marked NLT are from the Holy Bible, New Living Translation, copyright © 1996, 2004, 2007 by Tyndale House Foundation. Used by permission of Tyndale House Publishers, Inc., Carol Stream, Illinois 60188. All rights reserved.

Scripture quotations marked KJV are from the King James Version.

Cover artwork: Dawn Waters Baker (dawnwatersbaker.com)
Cover design: Frank Gutbrod
Interior design: { In a Word } (inawordbooks.com)
Proofreading: Line for Line Publishing Services

Library of Congress Cataloging-in-Publication Data

Names: Waters, Larry J., editor.
Title: When suffering is redemptive : stories of how anguish and pain accomplish God's
    mission / edited by Larry J. Waters ; foreword by Joni Eareckson Tada.
Description: Wooster : Weaver Book Company, 2016.
Identifiers: LCCN 2016003057 | ISBN 9781941337585
Subjects: LCSH: Suffering—Religious aspects—Christianity. | Consolation. |
    Redemption—Christianity. | Providence and government of God—Christianity.
Classification: LCC BV4909 .W485 2016 | DDC 248.8/6—dc23
LC record available at http://lccn.loc.gov/2016003057

Printed in the United States of America

16 17 18 19 20/ 5 4 3 2 1

Contents

Foreword

When I first leafed through the book you hold in your hands, two sentences quickly caught my eye: "Sometimes we are unwilling, shunning the very thing that will move [God's] redemptive purpose forward. That 'thing' is *suffering*."

In those few words, Larry Waters described me perfectly. Decades ago when I broke my neck in the diving accident that left me a quadriplegic, I couldn't have cared less about God's redemptive purposes. I hated life in a wheelchair. All I wanted was the use of my hands and legs. Yet when I finally found myself in a corner with nowhere else to turn, God suddenly became my "ever present help in trouble."

Nearly fifty years later, God is still backing me into corners. And in every one, I am still discovering fresh new levels of how tender and powerful His help is. Sometimes it involves battling stage III cancer or lung infections or dealing daily with chronic pain; whatever the case, I have come to know suffering. I have also come to know that my Savior is ecstasy beyond compare, and it is worth anything to be His friend.

Still, there are deeper levels of His grace to explore. That means more corners to be led into, especially as older age encroaches. Each new affliction exposes dark corners in my heart where peevishness and unwillingness still hide. My spirit can still dig in its heels when it comes to cooperating with God and His redemptive purposes. My will is still quick to crumble when pain heightens, and my emotions become too easily deflated when new afflictions loom.

This is why I make every effort to surround myself with people who inspire and encourage my weak heart—people who have stepped into the inner sanctum of sharing in Christ's sufferings and have not only survived, but flourished. I look for stories that enlarge my vision, invigorate my faith, and bolster my confidence in Christ. I dare not listen to my soul when I'm in pain; rather, I listen to the Bible-breathed words of courageous brothers and sisters in Christ who whisper, "Joni, you may think it's impossible, but you *can* do all things—even live with pain today—through Christ who strengthens you!"

I know this is why you'll enjoy—and more, be blessed by—reading *When Suffering Is Redemptive.* The remarkable testimonies in the following pages will refresh your weary heart and point you to God's purposes in your suffering. And that's a good thing. Because suffering is not as private and personal as you think. There is a divine mission to be accomplished through your afflictions—a Spirit-blessed mission where the cosmic stakes are about as high as you can get. Let *When Suffering Is Redemptive* elevate you onto that celestial battlefield alongside other valiant warriors, the place where you, too, will discover that the Lord is *always* your ever present help in trouble.

Joni Eareckson Tada
Joni and Friends International Disability Center,
Agoura Hills, CA

Preface

An agent of redemption is a person of courage, compassion, and conviction on mission with Jesus to turn what was intended for harm into good.[1]

For to you it has been granted for Christ's sake, not only to believe in him, but also to suffer for his sake. (Phil. 1:29, NASB)

Every day people ask the age-old question, "Why does God allow evil and suffering?" As human beings, we all struggle with this question at some point. We wonder how a loving and powerful God can allow suffering to leave its ugly mark on our bodies and souls, seemingly without His intervention.

For Christians these questions are not simple to answer because we believe that the Lord is actively involved in our lives. Especially puzzling is the problem of *undeserved suffering*—suffering that cannot be traced to any act of personal sin or disobedience. The authors in this book believe that God is on mission through our suffering to redeem this world.

But how is suffering redeemable? Can something so horrible and painful be compatible with the redemptive plan of God? Can we demonstrate triumph in the midst of our own undeserved suffering, proclaiming Christ's sovereign will and love for a world overwhelmed by war, death, violence, evil, and sin?

John Swinton writes that the problem of suffering is "primarily a practical

1 Albert L. Reyes, *The Jesus Agenda: Becoming an Agent of Redemption* (Dallas: Believers Press, 2015), 63.

problem that profoundly impacts [our] lives, the lives of [our] families, and [our] communities."[2] A practical problem requires a practical theology—a "critical, theological reflection on the practices of the church as they interact with the practices of the world, with a view to ensuring and enabling faithful participation in God's *redemptive* practices in and for the world."[3]

This is what this book hopes to accomplish. We want to use personal stories to illuminate biblical principles that will enable others to participate in the redemptive aspects of suffering. To a world that cannot make sense of the evil and sin in which it is immersed, we represent God's purpose through the inevitability of undeserved suffering.

To call suffering *undeserved* does not deny that humankind is justly under the curse as a result of the Fall as described in Genesis. Even so, suffering may be viewed as undeserved in the sense of being incompatible with pre-conceived or logical reasons for it; it may therefore appear unfair or unjust. Undeserved suffering, then, causes a person to consider deeper questions, especially as it affects the life of one who has a loving, intimate relationship with the true and living God. Questions that relate to God, man, and Satan, justice and injustice, sovereignty and freedom, God's power and our weakness, innocence and guilt, good and evil, and blessing and cursing are interlinked with the experience of undeserved suffering.

In these pages you will encounter regular people who have to struggle daily with undeserved suffering. You will meet a man who has faithfully served Christ for decades, but who as a young child watched his own father commit suicide. You will meet a woman whose experience raising a son with cerebral palsy led her to be deeply involved in major ministries for the disabled. A longtime servant of the homeless will inspire you to see people's inner hurts and introduce them to the one true Healer. You will read stories of chronic pain, of suicide and its effects, of the death of a child, and you will also encounter a Christian philosopher, who tackles the hard questions related to suffering. These stories and more demonstrate the love and faithfulness of God in His redemptive work through suffering, disability, and pain.[4]

This book is not a theodicy. These stories do not seek to explain the *why* of suffering, but rather present *ways* that God can transform and redeem

---

2   John Swinton, *Raging with Compassion: Pastoral Responses to the Problem of Evil* (Grand Rapids: Eerdmans, 2007), 7.

3   Ibid. Emphasis mine.

4   Since some authors come from an academic background, their chapters contain more documentation than others. However, every effort has been made to make each chapter engaging and transformative.

suffering in the life of the individual and in the Christian community. The stories are personal, sometimes difficult to tell. The authors are transparent with their struggles and honest in their questions, yet they have not lost sight of Christ and His purpose for their lives.

The natural reaction to suffering is anger, confusion, and feelings of alienation from God. But the eventual end should be redemption—the faithful sufferer transformed for the glory of God. Is understanding necessary? No. Only by emphasizing the redemptive quality of suffering can we cope with the unexplainable. For those who are part of God's plan, suffering is the embodiment of Christ to those who do not believe in Him or who have lost confidence in God's purpose and ways.

Larry J. Waters

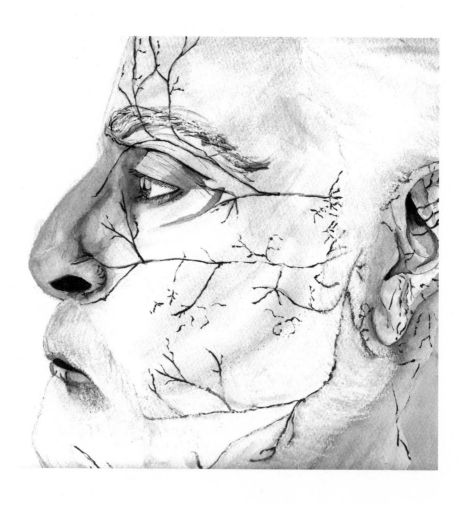

ONE

Redeeming the Worst Pain Known to Medical Science: My Suffering and the Mission of God

LARRY J. WATERS

> For this reason, *to keep me from exalting myself,* there was given me a thorn in the flesh, a messenger of Satan to torment me—*to keep me from exalting myself!* Concerning this I implored the Lord three times that it might leave me. And He has said to me, *"My grace is sufficient for you, for power is perfected in weakness.* (2 Cor. 12:7–9a, emphasis mine)[1]

It's nighttime. About an hour after drifting off to sleep, I suddenly awake with a painful, burning sensation in my left eye radiating into my sinus cavity. I try to shift positions and go back to sleep. The throbbing becomes nauseating. I plead, "Please, Lord, don't let this be another cluster headache."[2]

My left eye feels like it's being pushed out of my head. Clear fluid leaks from my left nostril. My left sinus cavity is blocked. I push up out of bed and stumble toward the kitchen, desperately trying to find medication. My left eyelid begins to shut; the pressure and pain keep building. I blink and the eye starts tearing. I'm going mad with pain, but I fumble in the cabinet for a glass and finally find one. I clumsily fill it with water and choke down the pill.

---

1   All Scripture quotations are from the NASB unless otherwise indicated.

2   Cluster headaches are characterized by an intense one-sided pain centered in the eye or temple. The pain lasts for one to two hours on average and may recur several times in a day. Cluster headaches have been known as histamine headaches, red migraines, and Horton's disease, among others.

My left cheek is covered with wetness. Is it blood, or just tears? I drop to the floor, stretch out full-length, and press my face onto the cold tiles hoping it will give me a moment without pain. I push my head down so hard I think the left side of my face will crack. I try sticking my head in the freezer or wrapping my face in ice packs. Always I'm hoping for relief. But there is none. I feel like I'm going insane. I cry out like a raving lunatic, begging God to stop the pain, asking Him to please take me home.

The cold floor and painkillers are not working. I pace from room to room, crying, flinging myself to the floor, getting up again, banging my head against the wall, squeezing my temples, all hoping for a moment of relief. Why isn't the medication working? I fall to my knees and pray again, begging the Lord to make this madness stop. The pain continues.

I try doing push-ups or pedaling on my stationary bicycle, hoping that will help the medicine work through my bloodstream faster. I'm willing to do anything to stop this excruciating, horrible, ghastly pain. Thirty minutes pass. I feel like my head will explode.

Mary, my wife, has been beside me the whole time, watching helplessly. She wants to help but can't. She sits beside me as I once again collapse on the floor, rocking back and forth. I'm whimpering like a lost little boy. She gets up, wraps an ice pack in a small towel, and kneels beside me, applying the towel to the left side of my face. She picks up my head slowly and rests it in her lap. She lovingly strokes my arms and my back. "Take a deep breath," she says. "Take another." I submit.

The medicine finally begins to work. The pain begins to subside, and like a demonic seizure, as suddenly as it began, it ends. I am exhausted. Mary helps me to the recliner and for the next two hours I pray that this terror called cluster headaches will not return. I wish I could say that my prayer has been answered. It has not. The pain still taunts, like a shadowy stalker pursuing its prey.

Dr. Anwarul Haq of the Baylor Neuroscience Center and Comprehensive Headache Center in Dallas, Texas, has referred to cluster headaches "as the worst pain known to man." After four days of IV treatments in his clinic to alleviate a cluster headache in August 2014, he explained that "the constant factor is that the pain transcends by far the distress of the more common tension-type headache or even that of a migraine headache. Women who have these pains have described them as worse than giving birth. It's officially and medically called the 'suicide headache.'"

The pain may strike three or four times a day. I will sometimes find relief for a few months after a surgical procedure, but the pain always returns. It is a malady that God has allowed me to have for seventeen years, evidently a necessary, permanent utility for my learning about God's mission through suffering. Is it something that I need to keep my arrogance controlled so that God's mission can move forward in my ministry? Paul spoke of his "messenger from Satan"—"his thorn in the flesh"—that helped his ministry to be more effective. Is this my thorn?

Paul may have been satisfied with God's answer, but even as a professor of Bible, I struggle with God's assurance that "My grace is sufficient for you, for power is perfected in weakness." Somehow, this never really connects with me when the "thorn" attacks. Any reassurance that "God's grace is sufficient," even from a beloved friend, just doesn't relate when pain invades my day or sleep.

However, as I will explain, I have come to understand that when these terrible spells pound my face, God is present with me advancing His mission through my pain. He is like Mary wrapping my head in ice, rocking me and soothing me with her voice and touch. God wraps His arms around me, comforts, soothes, and encourages me with His Word, assuring me that my suffering is vital to His mission, that His grace truly *is* sufficient and absolutely essential for His plan to be accomplished in my life.

Nevertheless, even as I complain about my disability, I recall that the most unlikely story in history is the mission of God to redeem humankind from sin and eternal punishment. How the Son of God could come into this world, live a perfect life, die for the sins of humanity, be buried, and rise from the grave victorious over death and Satan, thereby providing redemption and eternal salvation for all who believe—this is the greatest story ever told—truly. That the second member of the Trinity suffered unimaginable torture and physical agony on the cross when our sins were poured out on Him and judged should stop all objectors who say, "God doesn't understand my suffering." John Piper writes thus:

> The suffering of the utterly innocent and infinitely holy Son of God in the place of the utterly undeserving sinners to bring us to everlasting joy is the greatest display of the glory of God's grace that ever was, or ever could be. Everything leading to it and everything flowing from it is explained by it, including all the suffering in the world.[3]

---

3   John Piper, "The Suffering of Christ and the Sovereignty of God," in *Suffering and the Sovereignty of God*, ed. John Piper and Justin Taylor (Wheaton, IL: Crossway, 2006), 82.

The Mission of God Defined

Missio Dei (mission of God) is a Latin phrase that "focus[es] our attention on God's redemptive purpose and action in human history."[4] "In a sense, we might think of God the Father as the sender, and both God the Son and God the Spirit as the divine missionaries. . . . Both are the ministering hands of God to bring humankind to salvation and into the family of God."[5]

As God's children we are the instruments used to forward His mission. Sometimes we are unwilling, shunning the very thing that will move His redemptive purpose forward. That "thing" is *suffering*. Redemptive suffering illustrates that the believer's suffering should be viewed as *an unparalleled opportunity to witness to God's goodness, justice, grace, and love to a world that is both believing and nonbelieving.* I would suggest that *God is on mission* through the lives of all who "suffer for His sake," because "it is God who is at work in you, both to will and to work for His good pleasure" (Phil. 2:13). However, that suggestion is much easier to make than to accept and apply when severe tragedy, suffering, or disability invades our lives. Redemptive suffering hears from individuals who have discovered how to live out the mission of God in such challenging times.

The Mission of God Disclosed in Redemptive Suffering

Redemptive suffering comes from men and women who have found the courage to tell their unlikely stories of participating in God's mission in their suffering, "filling up what is lacking in Christ's afflictions" (Col. 1:24, ESV). To be sure, there is no deficiency in the work of Christ on the cross for our salvation. Rather, "filling up what is lacking" refers to the ongoing suffering of believers who exemplify Christ in and through that suffering for the sake of moving forward the mission of God and His gospel. As God's image-bearers, the authors in this volume see their genuine need to be brought to a place of loving obedience to God's plan. They accept that this plan, which cannot be improved or bypassed, includes suffering. In fact, His Word says,

---

4   Mark Young, "*Missio Dei* in Evangelicalism" (unpublished work, Dallas Theological Seminary, 2007), 1.

5   See J. Scott Horrell, "The Trinity, the *Imago Dei*, and the Nature of the Church" in *Connecting for Christ: Overcoming the Challenges Across Cultures,* ed. Florence Poh-Lian Tan (Singapore: Poh-Lian Tan, 2009).

"It has been granted to you that for the sake of Christ you should not only believe in him but also suffer for his sake" (Phil. 1:29, ESV).

As unlikely as it may seem, such stories are often the most effective witness of saving and living faith to the unbelieving world around us. Why? Because these writers of this book have liberated suffering, *freeing it to give glory to God.* God is on mission through their pain, sorrow, weakness, or disability to show the world what Christ can do through a life totally given to Him.

NOT SIN BUT

The Mission of God Discovered through Undeserved Suffering
GOD's MISSION!

It may well be that the undeserved suffering[6] in the life of a believer is a primary witness for God to our sin-sick world. The Gospels clearly show that no sin of Christ's own doing led Him to suffer. The blindness of the man in John 9 did not result from his sin or the sin of his parents (vv. 1–3). Paul suffered for God's purpose in keeping him humble (2 Cor. 12:7–12) and endured many other difficulties for Christ's sake (2 Cor. 11:23–28). The faith heroes of Hebrews 11 suffered not because of sin but for God's mission.

I first encountered this truth when I met a man from the land of Uz by the name of Job. His story is the classic example of how God's mission moves forward in spite of undeserved suffering. Job's life reveals the redemptive purpose of the Triune God working through the undeserved suffering of this one individual for the furtherance of His mission. Job's discovery of God's mission and grace helped me understand how God uses personal loss and pain in my own life.

From Job's unlikely story, I discovered that *suffering* and *pain* are also *grace!* Suffering has produced things in my life that nothing else could accomplish. Without it, my life might have turned down many wrong roads. Humility, witnessing opportunities, comfort and compassion toward others, and dependence on the Lord are only a few of the qualities and doors opened by my pain. I understand so much more about God than I would have without the grace of suffering. I learned about God's *sovereignty*, that my life is under the control of the Creator God, who sustains life and uses His servants in ways that we might not, and probably would not, choose. I understood

---

6   As noted in the introduction, "undeserved suffering" does not deny that humankind is justly under the curse as a result of the Fall in Genesis 3. Nor does it imply that anyone is sinless or without sin during one's lifetime. Rather, it refers to suffering that is not traceable to an act of personal sin or disobedience in the life of the believer. It is undeserved in the sense of being incompatible with preconceived or logical reasons.

more about God's *infinity*, that He cannot be understood or boxed in by my ideas about him. I immersed myself in a study of God's *eternality*, for His blessing and grace for my life are not limited to the short time I have on this earth. I may and do want relief from pain NOW, but for His purpose and His mission, I can wait until eternity. Understanding these three attributes—sovereignty, infinity, and eternality—moved me from a focus on myself and my suffering to the infinite God whose purposes and mission are eternal and who knows exactly what He is doing with this weak life of mine (2 Cor. 12:9).

Job's Discovery of God's Mission

When we read the book of Job, we are immediately drawn to the integrity and virtue of the main character. Job was "blameless, upright, fearing God, and turning away from evil" (1:1). The book's author considered Job to be the "greatest of all the men of the east" (1:3), and God said of Job that "there is no one like him on the earth" (1:8).

How does Job's undeserved suffering advance the mission of God? How is God "on mission" through the unmerited suffering in this human example? If Job's greatness included being well known during his own time in history, then his experiences were "front-page news," influencing untold others in his own day and certainly throughout history. Centuries later, James was able to say, "We count those blessed who endured. You have heard of the endurance of Job and have seen the outcome of the Lord's dealings, that the Lord is full of compassion and is merciful" (James 5:11).

Satan, God, and Job

Following the introduction of God's man, Job, this unlikely story takes the reader into the very throne room of God: "Now there was a day when the sons of God came to present themselves before the LORD, and Satan also came among them" (1:6). God took the initiative[7] to introduce Job into the conversation with Satan for the purpose of moving this unlikely story forward. God would use the suffering and pain of "the greatest man on earth" to reveal himself to Job's world. God was introducing two biblical concepts that

---

7   This is not to imply that God did not know what Satan had been doing or what his intent was. God asks the question to draw the reader into the narrative. A helpful discussion is found in Susannah Ticciati, "Does Job Fear God for Naught?," *Modern Theology* 21, no. 13 (July 2005): 353–66.

are normally contradictory to our thinking but are intricately connected: *grace* and *suffering*. The book of Job shows how these two concepts revolutionize our thinking about their relationship to advancing the mission of God in our lives.

Satan asked God two questions: "Does Job fear God for nothing?" and "Have You not made a hedge about him and his house and all that he has, on every side?" (1:9–10). Satan accused Job of worshiping God for what he materially gets out of the relationship. More directly, Satan implied that God *buys* worshipers through protection and material prosperity. If God did not protect, prosper, and promote Job, then Job would not worship Him. The challenge is to allow Satan the opportunity to prove his accusations.

Is Job's and, by implication, our relationship with God based on ease of life and prosperity? Is God a puppet who can be manipulated through a good life and virtuous works? Is God so impotent that He must purchase human worship through materialism, protective walls of defense, and grants of prosperity? Is the God of Job like all the other gods of the ancient world, who operated on a quid pro quo, an "I-please-you-and-you-please-me" system of theology? Or is the God of Job free to bless based on His own will and grace to accomplish His mission totally for His own glory?

If God's work could be reduced to a quid pro quo system, then God would be no different from the false gods of the ancient Near East. Scripture maintains that God does not punish or reward on the basis of human terms. Therefore we cannot accept the proposition that God acts unjustly or that He is controlled by human stimulus. According to God's Word suffering has many purposes, all of which fall under the governance of the justice and holiness of God. To think otherwise diminishes God to "a god" and exaggerates suffering beyond its importance, where all things revolve around its existence or absence. Therefore *the undeserved suffering of Job (and of sufferers today) is the battlefield, where the accuser (Satan) and the Accused (God) decide such questions.*

Again, this is a lesson I had a difficult time learning. I blamed myself for everything that went wrong in my life and the life of my family. I often blamed God, spiritually shaking my fist in His face and demanding, like Job, that He explain Himself to me. I even felt as Job did in chapter 3, that I would rather not have been conceived, and if conceived, stillborn.

I had to discover one of the primary messages of the book of Job: that grace is truly unmerited favor active in *both* pain and promotion, in *both* blessing and suffering. Once I learned this, my life with God became sweeter and more intimate. I felt closer to God in times of intense head pain, struggles with finances, and the loss of a child than in any time He was prospering me. Oh, I still questioned, cried out, and felt abandoned at times, but those glitches would move into an intimacy that was sweeter and more cherished than any cure or material blessing.

Yes, it is hard to understand. Yet I know that in eternity I will be cured, I will share material blessing beyond my imagination, and we will have our child with us forever. The "fellowship of God is enriching, and . . . that fellowship may be found in adversity no less than in prosperity."[8] Suffering is therefore the channel through which God dispenses His grace and love in a remarkable way and where His attributes, His character, and His love are more clearly manifest to the sufferer—to me.

We will soon dive more deeply into the insidious attack of Satan on God and His grace, and into the true reason Job and those of us like him worship God. First, let's look at the actions of Satan and his disdain for God's people. How does Satan use pain and suffering to try and draw the people of God away from God's mission?

The Mission of God Demonstrated

Devin Lee

"You have a son!" declared the nurse, "and your wife is fine." What joy filled our hearts. We were new missionaries, just five months in our host country. After nine months of anticipation, my mind was flooded with a father's dreams of football, baseball, fishing, and passing on our family name. Mary's heart looked ahead to what he would become, whom he might marry, to grandchildren, and a relationship that only mothers and sons enjoy.

Mary's pregnancy had been difficult. She had fallen several times, and the stress of deputation, raising funds, traveling throughout the United States, and sleeping in different beds almost every night had been grueling. After more than a year of this, she suffered an arduous four-week trip by freighter to the Philippines.

What we had thought would be a time of rest and recovery wasn't. The trip included a weeklong typhoon, long days of seasickness, and more stress due to pregnancy. This terrible ordeal for Mary was a delightful adventure

---

8   H. H. Rowley, "The Intellectual versus the Spiritual Solution," in *The Dimensions of Job: A Study and Selected Readings*, ed. Nahum N. Glatzer (New York: Schocken, 1969), 126.

for our three-year-old daughter DeAnna, who viewed the trip as a lark. Watching her toys move from one side of the cabin to the other during the typhoon, she would squeal with delight as drawers flew out of the cabinets and across the room. For her, the storm was more fun than a roller-coaster at Disneyland. Her little buggy where her dolls slept rolled back and forth across the room. What fun!

For Mary, however, it was torture. We had not listened to wiser voices telling us to postpone our trip overseas until the baby was born. We felt that we had to demonstrate our commitment and value as dedicated missionaries. We were driven, thinking that the cause of Christ could not wait, that God would take care of Mary and the baby.

We settled in a region of the Philippines that was rather primitive by United States standards. Although medical treatment was adequate, the care and facilities were unsophisticated. But since we were expecting a normal delivery, we were not particularly concerned. Devin was born on December 14. Almost immediately, complications developed. Devin was placed in an incubator. The doctors repeatedly took him in and out of the incubator over a three-week period. This was a mistake. The constant changes from the controlled atmosphere of the incubator to the tropical heat of the recovery room resulted in pneumonia as well as other serious respiratory problems.

Long hours looking through a window stretched into days. Our son put up a valiant fight, but after nearly a month of life, Devin was dying. Mary and I were finally allowed to touch him for the first time since the day of his birth. As we held his little hands, Devin slipped into the arms of Jesus on January 12.

After Devin's death we made preparations for the funeral. I was required to go to a local funeral parlor to arrange for Devin's burial. Forget all you know about American funeral arrangements. The gentleness and protocol of the American funeral and burial process did not exist in that place—not that day. A tiny casket was brought in for my approval. The best they had was poorly constructed of cheap wood, whitewashed, and fitted for a small Filipino baby. I commented that it was too short for Devin's body. With the strong odor of liquor on his breath the owner simply replied, "Oh, never mind, we will just break his legs and bend them underneath him." Sickened and appalled, I insisted on a larger and more appropriate casket and did not leave until one was supplied. No words could describe the revulsion and horror I faced at the prospect of leaving our son's body in that alien environment. Still, it had to be done. I thanked God that Mary was not with me that day.

The funeral was a kind and gentle affair. Missionaries, Filipino pastors, their congregations, and many friends all paid their respects. The Filipino believers wept with us and felt our pain. Many had lost their own children; they whispered as they embraced us that they understood how we felt, and they did.

But soon after the funeral the anger and self-loathing began. I could not see God on mission through our son's death. I blamed myself for my decision to leave the United States. I was also mad at God for not protecting us. I was depressed, confused, and full of questions. How could this be happening? Why was our heavenly Father displeased with us? Were we being punished for some decisions we made? Mary and I were not perfect, but we were good people. We were missionaries. We had sacrificed, surrendered, left family and friends, endangered our lives, lived on a small salary, and responded faithfully to the call of God. So why did God allow this to happen? What did taking our son have to do with the mission of God? What I didn't understand at the time, or couldn't understand in my grief, was that the mission of God was directly connected to how we responded to the suffering associated with Devin's death.

As the weeks and months went by this event more than any other drove us to the Scriptures in an attempt to discover how Devin's death mattered to God's mission for our lives. Only in His Word would we come to understand how the mission of God could exist in the confusion of such intense suffering. We had to find answers.

Loss of Children

"While he [a messenger to Job] was still speaking, another also came and said, 'Your sons and your daughters were eating and drinking wine in their oldest brother's house, and behold, a great wind came from across the wilderness and struck the four corners of the house, and it fell on the young people and they died, and I alone have escaped to tell you'" (Job 1:18–19).

The most troubling of Job's losses is Satan's murder of his ten children. The death of a child is unspeakably difficult in any family; in the ancient world the loss of children also meant the loss of future provision, as children were the "social security" of the elderly. Emotionally, Job was grief-stricken over the loss of his children (1:20–21), lost his sense of inner tranquility (3:26), lost his taste for life (3:1–4), was depressed (3:24–25), experienced troubled thoughts (7:4, 13–14), felt uncertain (9:20), was without joy (9:25; 30:31), and suffered from loneliness (19:13–19). His three friends implied that

Job's sin had caused the death of his children (5:4; 21:19; 27:14). Spiritually, Job was distressed over his conflict with a system of thought that could only conclude that God was an unpredictable tyrant who delights in afflicting His servant (6:4; 7:17–19; 30:11). He accepted God's sovereignty in the loss of his wealth and children, but he eventually questioned God's goodness and justice.[9] During Devin's short life, my wife and I experienced many of these emotions and experiences, and at times we, too, questioned God's goodness and justice.

I realize that a strong case can be made that we all deserve the suffering we experience. The effects of original sin and our continual choices as the human race against a relationship with God stand witness to our fallen condition. It is certainly true that rebellion and sin against God have consequences (Rom. 5:12; Gen. 2:17; 3:15–17). War, child abuse, prejudice, oppression, and all the evil that humans do result from their rebellion against God and His plan. Humankind chose to separate itself from God's life-source. The results are recorded in human history.

So one of the purposes for suffering is to punish our sin—not to drive us away from God, but to drive us to Him and into the arms of a forgiving Father (Heb. 12:5–6; Prov. 3). The answer to suffering for sin is to confess and repent, to believe in the Lord and find favor with Him (Prov. 28:13). Job and his friends understood this aspect of theology, but the three friends wrongly applied it to Job's situation. Not all suffering is related to personal sin. By the way, the descendants of those three friends are alive and well on planet Earth today, ready to remind us that all suffering is related to some personal sin, evil, or disobedience.

Mary and I struggled after Devin's death, even failed at times, but we

---

9 John E. Hartley, *The Book of Job*, New International Commentary on the Old Testament (Grand Rapids: Eerdmans, 1988), 47–48. Hartley shows that Job's suffering involved "every dimension of his existence—physical, social, spiritual, and emotional." So agrees Roy B. Zuck, "A Theology of the Wisdom Books and the Song of Songs," in *A Biblical Theology of the Old Testament*, ed. Roy B. Zuck (Chicago: Moody Press, 1991), 227. Zuck points out where the following "four dimensions of suffering" are seen in the book: (a) physical, 1:13–14; 2:8–10, etc.; (b) social, 2:7–8; 19:13–19 (alienated from family); 6:14–23 (disloyalty of friends); 16:10; 30:1–15 (taunt songs); (c) spiritual, 6:4; 7:17–19; 19:25; 23:8–9, 15; and (d) emotional, 3:26; 7:4, 11, 13–14; 9:2, 20, 28; 10:1–3; 12:4; 19:13–19; 21:6; 27:2 (Roy B. Zuck, *Job*, Everyman's Bible Commentary [Chicago: Moody Press, 1978], 15–19). Zuck discusses the losses and suffering of Job in some detail, pointing to such skin conditions as leprosy, smallpox, psoriasis, pityriasis, keratosis, and pemphigus foliaceus (ibid.). Also see A. Rendle Short, *The Bible and Modern Medicine* (Chicago: Moody Press, 1953), 6–61; and C. Raimer Smith, *The Physician Examines the Bible* (New York: Philosophical Library, 1950), 60.

knew nothing we had done previously was related to these sufferings. We had committed no sin to confess, no evil to repent of, and we had no reason to continue condemning ourselves. I returned to my study of the book of Job. There we discovered that Job also had suffered great emotional and spiritual pain at the loss of his children, a loss experienced for no reason commensurate with his personal life. I kept studying this man's life, delving more into his intense suffering.

Material and Financial Suffering

God takes the initiative (1:8; 2:3) to introduce His servant into an unspeakably painful battle with the accuser. God's questions to Satan, "Where have you been?" and "Have you considered my servant Job?," are not questions of a limited God with deficient knowledge. God knows where Satan has been and whom he wants to attack. Even though Satan has to ask permission, he is allowed to attack God's hero with a viciousness and rapidity that are almost beyond comprehension. Would God's relationship with Job demonstrate that a person could lose everything and yet continue to worship the Lord? As the attacks unfold in the narrative of chapter 1, the phrase "while he was still speaking" (1:16, 17) tells the reader that several catastrophic things happened to Job within minutes (vv. 13–21).

Job suffered a total financial collapse. A Sabean raiding party rustled all of Job's donkeys and oxen; fire fell from the heavens and consumed his sheep; a Chaldean raiding party rustled all of his camels. In each case, only one servant escaped, left with the harsh task of informing Job. In a world where wealth was measured in livestock and people, everything Job owned was gone in a few moments. Like Job, you may be suffering the loss of material and financial blessing and stability. But God is on mission through financial loss, personal failure, job loss, and the insecurity we feel when everything looks desolate.

The Honda Incident

The years 2001 and 2002 were among the most financially stressful periods of our marriage. We were starting over in the United States after a forced return from the Philippines. After twenty-seven years of missionary service, my cluster headaches sent us home to seek treatment. We were barely making it on the salary I made as an adjunct instructor teaching night classes at Dallas Theological Seminary (DTS) and Criswell College. We sought out doctors to help with my headaches, but no insurance company would cover the necessary medicine and treatments for my "preexisting illness." We experimented with drug therapy until, months later, an operation loomed on the horizon. It would cost thousands of dollars, but once again, we had no insurance coverage. We prayed the doctors would allow a payment schedule, but we were prepared to face any cost if there was a chance of stopping the attacks. Meanwhile, my mother was seriously ill in the hospital with pneumonia; the doctors weren't sure if she would make it. She, too, needed financial assistance.

After a long night class at DTS, I walked out to the faculty parking lot at 9:30 pm to find that my five-year-old Honda was missing. After a campus-wide search with a security guard, I came to the awful conclusion that no, this was not just another case of an absent-minded professor forgetting where he had parked. The car had indeed been stolen. We reported it to the Dallas Police Department. My immediate concern was for how we could get back and forth to visit my mother and at the same time make it to work. Then I remembered that the car was insured and that we would probably get a newer used car within a few days. For a time, I actually hoped the Honda would not be found.

But three days later, it was. I arrived at the police station to find the inside gutted; my tools, radio, and more were gone. The front end was badly damaged, as were the right side and rear end. Maybe it will be totaled, I hoped. I didn't want to wait for several weeks while it was being repaired. "Not totaled," the Honda technicians told me. "We can fix this." I groaned, disappointed. For the next two months we shuffled between the hospital and the two schools, using all our extra funds for Mother's medication and bills. However, I finally drove away in a beautifully remade 1997 Honda that served me well for the next few years.

A few months after the accident, I received an official-sounding phone call telling me to appear in court the next week. Shocked, I asked why. I was informed that they had caught the person who had stolen my car and that if I wanted to file for damages or loss, I should come to court and give my estimate to the judge. Recovery of $1,500 was possible.

I had never been in court and knew little of the procedures, so I called a close friend, a Christian lawyer, and asked him to show me the ropes. Attorney Ray North agreed to help me. He added that, as was his custom, he would take several wooden crosses, which he carved as a hobby, plus a bundle of tracts by Roy Zuck titled *The Cross*, just in case we had a chance to witness. I took the hint and brought a box of *More Than a Carpenter* by

Josh McDowell, a short book presenting Christ as the promised Messiah and Savior.

When we arrived and entered the anterooms where the defense and prosecution lawyers met, I looked into the room reserved for the defense and saw the young man who had stolen my car. His mother sat beside him. Both were frightened and weeping loudly. I looked at my friend Ray and said simply, "I can't do this; $1,500 doesn't mean that much to me." I asked Ray and the defense lawyer if they would allow me to drop the charges, with one condition: that the young man would read the book by McDowell and then give a book report to the court. The lawyers laughed and said, "That sounds like a professor!" But they didn't think the judge would agree. After I begged them, they timidly went into the courtroom to present the proposition to the judge.

As she listened to the request, the judge turned her head and looked toward me. I was sure I detected a scowl. She then motioned and called all of us into a full courtroom. Along with Ray, the defense lawyer, the young man, and his mother, we all stepped up to the bench. The judge looked at me and forcefully asked, "What's this book you want this young man to read?" I calmly replied, "It's a book about Jesus Christ and how to trust him as personal Savior. I want the young man to consider becoming a Christian." She turned to the young man and said very sternly, "Young man, you will read this book, and report back to me with a book report in three weeks! Is that clear?" He nodded sheepishly, "Yes, ma'am." The judge then turned to me looking sternly over her reading glasses and, with a twinkle in her eyes, asked, "Is that what you wanted?" I respectfully replied, "Yes, Judge, and thank you!" She struck her gavel loudly and announced, "Case dismissed."

As we turned to leave the courtroom, I felt a tug on my sport coat. "May I have one of those books?" the court recorder asked. I gladly gave her one. As I walked on I felt another tug at my coat. "I'd like one too," said the security guard. Before I was out of the courtroom all of the books were given out. As Ray and I went into the hallway we noticed several people had been watching the proceedings. Many more asked me for books, but I had given them all away. Ray said, "No problem," and started handing out dozens of wooden crosses (necklaces and bookmarks) along with Roy Zuck's *The Cross* tract. Before we left the courthouse we handed out everything we had. We floated out to the parking lot with tears in our eyes, thanking the Lord for letting us be part of His mission for that day. God acted for His glory. But that's not the end of the story.

One year later, the young man's attorney (who we learned was also a believer in Christ) met my friend Ray in the hallway at juvenile court. He told Ray that the young man and his mother had both received Christ as Savior, were baptized, and were now attending a Bible-believing church! That little Honda was an instrument used by God to bring others to Him. And though my mother finally recovered, our finances didn't improve a great deal, and no permanent job was on the horizon. But the honor of being a part of God's mission made us rich beyond measure. We saw personally that God's mission continues even when we have little or nothing materially to offer or sustain us.

Physical Suffering

Job had already lost all of his material wealth and all of his children. Still, over the next few months (7:3; 29:2), his personal suffering increased. He suffered physical pain and disease that included inflamed, ulcerous boils (2:7), itching (2:8), degenerative changes in facial skin (2:7, 12), loss of appetite (3:24), insomnia (7:4), hardened skin, running sores, worms in the boils (7:5), difficulty breathing (9:18), weight loss (16:8), eye difficulties (16:16), emaciation (17:7; 19:20), bad breath (19:17), trembling of the limbs (21:6), continual pain in the bones (30:17), restlessness (30:27), blackened, peeling skin (30:28, 30), and fever (30:30).[10]

Physical suffering is a major area of spiritual attack. Someone has said that if Satan cannot solicit through prohibited pleasure ("Why wait on God's plan and will?"), he will solicit through pain ("How could a loving God allow such a thing?"). Satan uses pain to drive a child of God into the twisted, confused maze of a life without God and His Word. As you read this, you may be suffering physical pain similar to one or more areas of Job's suffering. Yet God is on mission through your pain, as I am discovering daily in my own journey with pain.

Social Suffering

Job also suffered socially. He lost his high status within the community and was alienated from family and friends. Job's loving wife caved under the pressure (2:9); he was rejected, jeered, and mocked by friends (12:4; 16:10; 17:2, 6), even by children (30:1, 9–11).[11] He was called a fool (5:2, 3); sinful

---

10   Zuck, "A Theology of the Wisdom Books and Song of Songs," 227.
11   Ibid.

(5:7; 18:5–22; 22:5–11); arrogant (8:2; 11:4, 7; 15:11–16; 18:3); evil (11:13; 15:20; 22:5); idle and useless (11:2); stupid (11:11–12); empty (15:2); unteachable (15:8–9); a byword, or object of scorn (17:6; 30:9); ugly (19:17–20); dishonest (20:19); a persecutor of widows and orphans (22:9); and a worm, scab, or maggot (25:6). Even today, those who suffer chronic illness, disability, or some form of visible affliction are ostracized, overlooked, and avoided. You will read stories like this in this book. But once again God is on mission even when you are marginalized. His plan for you is not hindered by the pain inflicted by the evil one.

Few have suffered as broadly and severely as Job, yet many, if not all, have suffered in one or more of these categories. The reason for listing Job's types of suffering is to establish that suffering is allowed by God and a reality in the often unknown and unexplainable "contest" or conflict with Satan. It also opens the key question: Can all of these categories of suffering move forward the mission of God?

The Mission of God Detailed: The Sufficiency of Grace

If suffering is allowed by God, and if it is part of the conflict with evil and the evil one, then it would seem likely that suffering is used by God in answering the lies of the evil one and the assumptions connected with his lies. A proper response to suffering would then lead to triumphing over the enemy's accusations and reaching the world with His message of grace. Clearly, Job's initial response exemplified this thinking:

> Then Job arose and tore his robe and shaved his head, and he fell to the ground and *worshiped.* He said, "Naked I came from my mother's womb, and naked I shall return there. The LORD gave and the LORD has taken away. Blessed be the name of the LORD." Through all this Job did not sin nor did he blame God. (Job 1:20–22, emphasis mine)

Later, when his wife urged that he give up and die, Job displayed a clear understanding of God's grace and the importance of handling suffering in light of that grace: "'Shall we indeed accept good from God and not accept adversity?' In all this Job did not sin with his lips" (2:10).

This is one of the most exceptional verses in the book of Job. It reveals a clear understanding of God's grace and the importance of handling suffering in light of that grace. Grace is normally defined as unmerited divine assistance given humans for their regeneration or sanctification, or, more simply, getting what we don't deserve. This would include both (1) undeserved blessing from God, and (2) undeserved pain and suffering.

Grace for the believer is sufficient in both blessing and in adversity. Why? Because the Lord is present with the one receiving grace—whatever form it may take. This is true for all of us who follow in similar circumstances. Job was to be a witness of God's grace in adversity. Witnessing, remember, involves more than just presenting the gospel to the unbeliever through written or verbal communication. Witnessing includes injecting biblical principle into life by example. When we suffer, God uses us to communicate His purpose and mission to others. We witness through our stories, pain management, and exemplary attitude. As the following chapters demonstrate, the most effective witnesses of Christ throughout history, then and now, have been suffering saints. Even though Job did not epitomize or demonstrate this witness consistently, he never let go of his belief that all things come from God and that ultimately it was to God alone that he could turn. Sometimes the only answer to our suffering is that God is the only answer. This is embodied in Job's final declaration: "I had heard of you by the hearing of the ear, but now my eye sees you" (42:5, ESV).

Job learned that God requires a relationship with His people based solely on grace (40:4; 42:5–6). Often only those who suffer undeservedly teach and learn this lesson. The famous statement of 42:5 helps us observe two things: "The first is that mere hearing in the sense of 'hearing of [or about]' is not sufficient. . . . The second observation is that true hearing and vision belong together. . . . To hear God is to see God. It is because Job has listened to God that he now sees God."[12] "This seeing was spiritual insight, not a physical vision. . . . Having deeper insight into God's character—His power, purposes, and providence—Job gained a more accurate view of his own finitude."[13] This would have been impossible without Job's adversity.

Job had "seen God," which means he had an immediate encounter with God that was unprecedented in its immanence. Job had not been crushed by the arrival of the divine presence as he had feared (9:17), but he had been overcome. He was unable to answer, just as he had anticipated (9:15), but he could not say he had not been heard (9:16). He was not as right as

12   Robert S. Fyall, *Now My Eyes Have Seen You: Images of Creation and Evil in the Book of Job* (Downers Grove, IL: InterVarsity Press, 2002), 179.

13   Zuck, *Job*, 184.

he assumed (9:15), for the questions of justice were more than he knew.[14] "God had met him face to face, and in the end that suited Job better than ten thousand answers."[15]

Job therefore understood the prosperity that was returned in chapter 42 as a gift from a gracious and loving God rather than as a deserved compensation for his own works (see chap. 31). This was a lesson I had to learn. For most of my Christian life I thought God blessed me because I deserved compensation for the good I was doing. I was wrong. Because of my lessons in the school of suffering, I was able to apply two principles.

First, I recognized a basic principle about sin: "I am unworthy . . . I put my hand over my mouth . . . I will say no more" (40:4, NIV). Second, I recognized the nature of God and responded with humility, love, and godly fear for God's sovereignty (as in 42:1–2). I realized God's inscrutability (42:3), reflected on God's superiority (42:4), refocused on God's intimacy (42:5), and repented of serving God from wrong motivations or presumption (42:6). Satan was silenced because Job's response (42:1–6) proved that God's confidence in him was not unfounded (1:8; 2:3). The book of Job taught me and my wife that God's confidence in us during suffering was not unfounded. We saw that God needs no vindication. Undeserved suffering, accepted and borne in faith by a child of God, does move God's gracious mission forward for His own glory and for the sake of His people. Mary and I had found answers that helped us through those dark nights of the soul.

The Mission of God: Personal Lessons

How does the mission of God apply to your life and mine? God taught me four things through the loss of our son, the Honda incident, and my cluster headaches. First, since the Fall of humankind (Gen. 3), God has never promised to eliminate suffering as a reward for believing in the Lord and becoming a Christian. Blessing is promised—and experienced—but it is not guaranteed during this life. Suffering is also promised (Phil. 1:29), and it is not eliminated until eternity. In fact, the *normal* life of one following the

---

14   August H. Konkel, "Job," in *Job, Ecclesiastes, Song of Songs*, Cornerstone Biblical Commentary 6 (Carol Stream, IL: Tyndale, 2006), 238.

15   Barbara Brown Taylor, "On Not Being God," *Review and Expositor* 99 (Fall 2002): 612.

command and will of the Lord involves both blessing and suffering (Job 2:10). This is evident both from Scripture and in modern life.

Second, suffering is often undeserved in the sense of not being related to any personal sin or bad decision on the part of the sufferer. Devin's death, our financial problems, and my terrible headaches are not related to any specific sins on our part.

Third, God in His sovereignty uses suffering for His own glory and purpose. Though He may not make His plans clear to the sufferer, at least not immediately, He still makes suffering effective for His own purpose.

Fourth, that purpose is the mission of God. That is, the suffering of God's own people moves the mission of God forward. This is the death knell for the prosperity gospel. The suffering of people like Abraham, Joseph, Paul, and many others has advanced the mission of God far more than easy lives ever could.

In the case of Job, knowledge of his suffering spread throughout the East, brought "wise men" to his side, drew curious onlookers into his argument with the three friends, and ultimately resulted in a witness of his relationship with the Lord. In our case, the loss of a child, the forgiveness of a criminal, and the experience of chronic pain have all opened doors for witnessing and counseling that would not have otherwise been unlocked. The biblical evidence shows that the mission of God is often founded on the personal life and experience of the one who believes in and trusts the Lord even during intense suffering.

While suffering allows for a powerful witness of faith in God, the mission of God in suffering also extends to the life and spiritual growth of the sufferer. In such times, God is working to teach, enhance, strengthen, refine, and mature the individual. I know this was the case in my own life. I will not know until eternity what sinful roads I might have taken, what evil decisions I would have made, were it not for the grace of God in undeserved suffering. My suffering directed me to His path and kept me on mission for Him. Eternal rewards and eternal relationships will eclipse any loss or pain we endure now.

In relation to the mission of God, the book of Job has a twofold purpose: (1) to correct a false doctrine that makes God "a capricious despot, who delights in afflicting his servant"[16] for no apparent reason (6:4; 7:17–19; 19:25); and (2) to impact the world with God's message of grace through His servant's experience.

---

16 Hartley, *The Book of Job*, 48.

In regard to the first purpose, van Zyl writes,

The book of Job had missiological implications for its own culture. It addressed a worldview according to which God was made subservient to human actions, and which, by implication, legitimized the position of the prosperous and powerful, and "demonized" the sick, the have-not's, the working class. . . . The book, through the laborious process of speeches, unmasks . . . this type of theology. . . . It brings hope to the poor and suffering that they may understand more of God than the wise do.[17]

What are the implications of the mission of God for those of us who suffer today? First, our emphasis during our suffering should be on *bringing the world into faith*.[18] The suffering believer has an untold opportunity to draw people to Christ. The attitude of the suffering believer determines the effect he or she will have on the unbeliever. While a negative response to suffering gives a poor witness for Christ, when we search for answers, we are often led to explanations that, when shared, influence and touch numerous lives for good.

For example, Joni Eareckson Tada's life and publications have not only encouraged and challenged others who have suffered and are suffering, but they have produced what is probably the most effective ministry to the disabled in history.[19] Elisabeth Elliot's loss of her husband and the death of four other missionaries in the Ecuadorian jungle resulted not only in the salvation of various tribal peoples, but influenced many—including me—to become missionaries.[20] Larry Crabb, who lost his brother in a tragic plane crash, documented his journey in trying to understand the purpose and mission of

---

17   Danie C. Van Zyl, "Missiological Dimensions in the Book of Job," *International Review of Mission* 91 (January 2002): 28.

18   Ibid., 24. Van Zyl identifies two major emphases in missions: "winning people from the world to faith" and "bringing the kingdom into the world" (emphasis removed). I alter these slightly but use the basic concepts.

19   Joni Eareckson Tada, *The God I Love: A Lifetime of Walking with Jesus* (Grand Rapids: Zondervan, 2003). Probably the best exposition of the principle above is in Joni Eareckson Tada and Steve Estes, *When God Weeps* (Grand Rapids: Zondervan, 1997).

20   Elisabeth Elliot, *Through Gates of Splendor* (Wheaton, IL: Tyndale, 1956). Elliot wrote many other books of significance that advance the *missio Dei* in the Christian world, among which are *Shadow of the Almighty* (New York: HarperCollins, 1989); *A Path Through Suffering: Discovering the Relationship Between God's Mercy and Our Pain* (Ventura, CA: Regal Books, 1990); and *The Savage My Kinsman* (Ventura, CA: Regal Books, 1996).

God through his brother's death.[21] Crabb's influence in biblical counseling has brought many to Christ. Martha Snell Nicholson prayed, "Dear Lord, illumine with Thy face each sick-room; make it, by Thy grace, an altar and a holy place."[22] She was an invalid for most of her life, confined to her bed. Yet God used her to write meaningful poetry that has touched many for the Lord. An example is "Treasures."

> One by one He took them from me,
>   All the things I valued most,
> Until I was empty-handed;
>   Every glittering toy was lost.
>
> And I walked earth's highways, grieving,
>   In my rags and poverty.
> 'Till I heard His voice inviting,
>   "Lift your empty hands to Me!"
>
> So I held my hands toward heaven,
>   And He filled them with a store
> Of His own transcendent riches,
>   'Till they could contain no more.
>
> And at last I comprehended
>   With my stupid mind and dull,
> That God could not pour His riches
>   Into hands already full.[23]

The second major emphasis during our suffering should be *bringing faith into the world*. Not only are we, through our suffering, given the opportunity to witness to the unbelieving world and influence others for Christ, but we also have the opportunity to demonstrate faith in God in spite of the suffering.

This is especially true during times of undeserved suffering—when there is no logical reason to trust a God who seemingly has forgotten us and offers

---

21   Larry Crabb, *Finding God* (Grand Rapids: Zondervan, 1995).

22   Martha Snell Nicholson, *Threshold of Heaven* (Wilmington, CA: printed by author, 1943), 1.

23   Martha Snell Nicholson, "Treasures," in *Ivory Palaces* (Chicago: Moody Press, 1949), 67.

no explanation for our anguish and agony. Probably the most common criticism of the Christian faith sounds something like, "How can a loving and powerful God allow such terrible and unjust suffering to exist?" Or as Bart Ehrman sadly confessed, "The problem of suffering has haunted me for a very long time. . . . Ultimately, it was the reason I lost my faith."[24]

These questions echo Satan's accusations in Job 1–2 that God is impotent and unjust. However, the believer who handles suffering in grace has the opportunity to make sense of the unexplainable and demonstrate confidence and faith in God despite these accusations. As Job's experience with undeserved suffering brought a timeless example of this to his world, so too can those of us who suffer teach that *a relationship with God, based on grace through faith, is the heart of all that really matters in our lives.* He is, after all, on mission to bring the world to faith in Him and to demonstrate faith through His servants to a lost and dying world. By sharing in His suffering, we participate in His mission.

Discussion Questions

1. If you feel you can, share with the group your story of how God used your life, your suffering, to move forward His mission.
2. Discuss your thoughts on the meaning of "God's grace is sufficient for you" not only from the experience of Job and Paul but also from your own experience.
3. How can you use your pain, suffering, or disability to bring the world to faith or to demonstrate faith to the world?
4. When has suffering reshaped your faith? How did "seeing" God instead of simply "hearing about" about God reshape your faith?
5. If God is the purpose of life, how does stripping us down to just Him help us find our purpose?

---

24   Bart D. Ehrman, *God's Problem* (New York: HarperCollins, 2008), 1.

Resources for Further Study

Books

Randy Alcorn, If God Is Good: Faith in the Midst of Suffering and Evil (Colorado Springs, CO: Multnomag, 2009).

Larry Crabb, *Finding God* (Grand Rapids: Zondervan, 1995).

Elisabeth Elliot, *Through Gates of Splendor* (Wheaton, IL: Tyndale, 1956).

———, *A Path Through Suffering: Discovering the Relationship Between God's Mercy and Our Pain* (Ventura, CA: Regal Books, 1990).

Linda Lawrence Hunt, *Pilgrimage Through Loss: Pathways to Strength and Renewal after the Death of a Child* (Louisville: Westminster John Knox Press, 2014).

John Piper, "The Suffering of Christ and the Sovereignty of God," in *Suffering and the Sovereignty of God*, ed. John Piper and Justin Taylor (Wheaton, IL: Crossway, 2006).

Joni Eareckson Tada and Steve Estes, *When God Weeps* (Grand Rapids: Zondervan, 1997).

Larry J. Waters, "A Biblical Theology of Suffering, Disability, and the Church," in iTunes University (under Dallas Theological Seminary).

Larry J. Waters and Roy B. Zuck, *Why, O God? Suffering and Disability in the Bible and the Church* (Wheaton, IL: Crossway, 2011).

Amos Yong, *The Bible, Disability, and the Church: A New Vision of the People of God* (Grand Rapids: Eerdmans, 2011).

Websites

The Cluster Headache Support Group Blog, chsg.org.; https://www.facebook.com/ClusterHeadacheSupport.

TWO

Redeeming a Life of Paralysis: Broken Wholeness

MARK R. TALBOT

> You have dealt well with your servant, O LORD.
> ... Before I was afflicted I went astray.
> ... You are good and do good.
> ... It is good for me that I was afflicted,
> that I might learn your statutes.
> The law of your mouth is better to me
> than thousands of gold and silver pieces.
> I know, O LORD, that your rules are righteous,
> and that in faithfulness you have afflicted me.
> (Psalm 119:65, 67, 68, 71–72, 75)

> I came that they may have life and have it abundantly.
> (John 10:10) [1]

When I was seventeen, I fell about fifty feet off a Tarzan-like rope swing, breaking my back and becoming paralyzed from the waist down.[2] I spent six months in two hospitals. Initially, I had no feel-

---

[1] All Scripture quotations are from the ESV unless otherwise indicated. All emphases are mine.

[2] Portions of this chapter are adapted from my forthcoming book, to be published by Crossway, titled, *When the Stars Disappear: Trusting God When We Suffer.* I am grateful to the Christian Scholars' Fund, who have supported my research and writing for the past

ing or movement in my legs and no bowel or bladder control. I dropped from 200 to 145 pounds because I got sick every time I ate. Once my back had stabilized a little and I had regained some leg movement, my physical therapist tried to help me regain more by having me crawl to breakfast. At the time, I had a calcified stone in my bladder that had formed when they had catheterized me for the first few weeks. The catheter had been removed, but the undetected stone remained. It was causing raging bladder infections. When they would put me on the floor each morning, I would wet myself and, because it was useless to change, remain soaked all day. The stone was finally detected and removed, and when I left the hospital a couple of weeks later I was able to control my bladder in most situations and walk awkwardly with one or two canes.

I am now sixty-five. My walking has become much slower, harder, and more painful, even with crutches. To walk more than fifty feet or to stand for more than a couple of minutes are now daunting prospects, yet I want to stay on my feet. I walk partly on muscle spasm, which raises my blood pressure, making it hard for me to find ways to exercise enough to stay in cardiovascular shape. I have to worry about things most people never even think about. In the last twenty years, I sometimes have had sleep-robbing leg spasms. And in the last ten years, my inability to walk much has depleted the bone density in my hips to the point where, if I take a really serious fall, they may break. Those falls happen more frequently now since my legs sometimes collapse unexpectedly.

Yet my accident is one of the three great blessings of my life. My body may be broken, but I am much more whole as a result.

Conversion

The greatest blessing of my life is my conversion, which took place when I was twelve.[3] I was frightened by some of my sins, and so when an evangelist made an appeal during a weekend retreat for young junior-high-school boys, I raised my hand, accepting Christ.

Initially, this gave me a new direction and some purpose and meaning. I began memorizing Scripture, and church and youth group became more important to me.

---

few years through their CSF Scholars program. This piece, with some additional footnotes, can be found on the Christian Scholars' Fund website at www.christianscholarsfund.org.

3   The third great blessing was God's providential provision of my wonderful wife, Cindy, and our daughter Kim.

Getting Focused

Yet through junior high and high school, I was floundering. As important as my conversion was, it didn't transform my day-to-day life. I had always had trouble relating to my peers, and that didn't change. My relationships with my teachers were often tense.

I fell in June, two days after the end of my junior year. My high school years had been disquieting. It was always clear I could succeed academically, if I would apply myself. But each day I would carry books home from school and never open them. Looking towards college, I had a gnawing sense of impending failure. I dreamed about experiences I thought college would bring, such as traveling with the University of Washington marching band, but I realized my aimlessness would probably mean I wouldn't survive my first year. I assumed I wouldn't finish college, but I had no idea what else I could do.

I frittered away my free time, living for inane experiences, like riding down sunny, winding country roads with my friends while listening to pop music or driving those roads by myself at breakneck speeds. My part-time jobs at boat docks and go-kart tracks increased my sense of life's basic meaninglessness, aggravating my *ennui*.

I sought my identity in risky and brash behavior that alienated me from my teachers and from God. My life seemed out of my control, which frightened me.

My fall's first blessing was that by suddenly cutting off a lot of possibilities, it focused me. Soon after hitting the ground, I saw that my legs were submerged in a little stream, yet I wasn't feeling anything. A few years before, I had met Brian Sternberg, who as a sophomore at the University of Washington in 1963 had twice broken the world record in the pole vault. That summer he had broken his neck when he lost his orientation while training on a trampoline. He became quadriplegic. As soon as I realized my legs weren't feeling anything, I knew that I had done something similar.

Yet, paradoxically, I immediately felt God's love for me. I knew that somehow this accident was from His hand and for my good.[4] Almost everything that had been distracting me fell away, and for the next several months I focused on just one thing: How much could I recover physically from my accident?

---

4   My sense of God's love for me immediately after my accident may seem more extraordinary than it actually is. I know of several instances where an inexplicable peace from God has followed immediately on some calamity (see Phil. 4:7). In my own case, there was nothing about me or what I believed at the time that could account for what I felt. It was simply God's gift.

Sensing My Dependence

I spent six weeks on a Stryker frame at Providence Hospital in Seattle. My mom spent each day with me, and then my father would come by after work and read me to sleep with Fulton Oursler's dramatization of our Lord's life in his *The Greatest Story Ever Told.* I then went to Good Samaritan Hospital's rehab center in Puyallup. Those were months without much Christian fellowship or Bible reading, but when I finally went home at Christmas, I regularly felt God's presence, especially after a fall.

By then I was in the habit of praying that God would help me with the most basic bodily tasks like urinating and standing and walking. I prayed during meals that nausea wouldn't keep me from eating. My precarious physiology drove home my need for God's mercies. Over the years my sense of dependence has increased as the difficulties have multiplied.

Of course, we all depend on God's sustaining hand, yet we easily forget this when we are flourishing. We assume we control our lives in ways we do not. At one point in His earthly ministry, our Lord warned His listeners against this assumption:

> Then he told them a story: "A rich man had a fertile farm that produced fine crops. He said to himself, 'What should I do? I don't have room for all my crops.' Then he said, 'I know! I'll tear down my barns and build bigger ones. Then I'll have room enough to store all my wheat and other goods. And I'll sit back and say to myself, "My friend, you have enough stored away for years to come. Now take it easy! Eat, drink, and be merry!"'
>
> "But God said to him, *'You fool! You will die this very night. Then who will get everything you worked for?'"* (Luke 12:16–20, NLT)

Making the same point in a slightly different way, James wrote this:

> Come now, you who say, "Today or tomorrow we will go into such and such a town and spend a year there and trade and make a profit"—yet *you do not know what tomorrow will bring.* What is your life? For you are a mist that appears for a little time and then vanishes. *Instead you ought to say, "If the Lord wills, we will live and do this or that."* As it is, you boast in your arrogance. All such boasting is evil. (James 4:13–16)

Good health and good fortune tempt us to think we are the masters of our own fate (see Deut. 8:11–14, 17-18). Regarding my health, this is a temptation I will never have to face.

Finding A New Delight

The psalmist who wrote Psalm 119 testified that his suffering led him to treasure God's words: "I used to wander off until you [afflicted] me; but now I [heed] your word. . . . My suffering was good for me, for it taught me to pay attention to your decrees" (vv. 67, 71, NLT). It has been the same for me.

For the first Christmas after my accident, my parents gave me what Oxford University Press called its Pilgrim Edition of the King James Version of the Bible. It had over 7,000 notes on the Scriptures, written so that they "might be helpful to any young Christians of any age."

Those notes opened the Scriptures for me. God's Word became my delight. I knew God was speaking to me through the words on the biblical pages. Looking at my worn copy now, I find I highlighted, underlined, and annotated some of the Old Testament and almost all of the New. Psalm 119:24 captures what I was experiencing: "Thy testimonies . . . are my delight and my counsellors" (KJV). I began to find my identity in Christ.

The psalmist's suffering led him to value God's words more than great wealth: "Your instructions are more valuable to me than millions in gold and silver" (v. 72, NLT). I found the lure of Scripture trumping even some of my stronger instincts. When I was in Good Sam, I found spending time with the female nursing students to be so attractive that I would allow them to practice drawing my blood. A few weeks after I got home, several of them drove sixty miles to our home to see how I was doing. But my delight in reading Scripture had become so intense that I excused myself after a few minutes, leaving them to talk with my parents as I went to read. Whenever I think about this, it makes me laugh: It seems that God and His Word *can* become more alluring than anything else!

Later trials and afflictions have repeatedly sent me to the Scriptures. When I had my first full-time position as a philosophy professor I became depressed because I was finding it difficult to finish my dissertation. Yet I found I had to open each morning with at least an hour of careful biblical study. Nothing else gave me the solace to go on.

Suffering Christians need to turn to the Scriptures, expecting God to meet them there. As I put it in a piece published in Seattle Pacific College's student newspaper early in my junior year, I had found that the pain of infirmity could not begin to touch the joy of closeness to Him.

Mark R. Talbot

Restored by Steadfast Love

The events recounted in the first chapter of the book of Ruth clearly constitute a personal calamity. Because of a famine in Judah, Elimelech took Naomi and their two sons to sojourn in Moab, where he died and the sons took Moabite wives. The sons then died before fathering children, and so Naomi was left a childless widow in a foreign land. In ancient times, this was perilous. Knowing this, she tried to dissuade her daughters-in-law from returning with her to Bethlehem (see 1:8-13).

As was customary with God's Old Testament people, Naomi took her suffering to have been divinely ordained, which she expressed in terms of "the hand of the LORD [having] gone out" against her, the LORD having "brought [her] back empty" to Bethlehem, the LORD having "testified against" her, as well as "the Almighty [having] brought calamity" upon her (1:13, 21).

Depending on how we construe the Hebrew, the women of Bethlehem's surprised "Is this Naomi?" upon her arrival back in her home village may suggest that Naomi's calamity had weighed so heavily on her that she was almost unrecognizable (1:19). In any case, given the significance of personal names in the ancient Near East, Naomi's reply, "Do not call me Naomi" (which means *pleasant*); "call me Mara" (which means *bitter*), "for the Almighty has dealt very bitterly with me" (1:20), shows she felt bitterness would characterize the rest of her life. For the entire time period covered in Ruth's first chapter, the woman whose name meant "pleasant" lost all hope her life would ever be pleasant again.

She was mistaken, as Ruth's last chapter shows. Naomi's inability in the midst of her suffering to hope her life could ever be pleasant again was no measure of God's ability to work out everything for her good. When she took Ruth's infant Obed into her arms at the story's end, her life was being restored by the same God who had made it so bitter. It became no irony to call her *Pleasant* again.

How did God restore Naomi's life? We are told in chapter 1 that He ended Israel's famine, prompting Naomi to get up and take to the road leading back to Judah (see 1:6-7). Then in Ruth's last chapter we read, "[T]he LORD gave [the previously barren Ruth] conception, and she bore a son" (4:13).

These two events bracket Naomi's story and thus emphasize two things.

First, they emphasize God's steadfast love for Naomi. By ending Israel's famine, He initiated the train of events that would restore her, even if she didn't know it then. Then, by giving Ruth conception, He opened the way for the event that would make her name appropriate again. For Obed's birth gave her a new lease on life. As the Bethlehem women exclaimed: "He will renew your life and sustain you in your old age" (4:15, NIV). And besides, they noted, she already was enjoying the great pleasure of Ruth's love: "For . . . your daughter-in-law . . . loves you and has been better to you than seven sons!"[5]

In the Hebrew Scriptures, God's steadfast love is called His *ḥesed*. This is a very rich word. Those who practice *ḥesed* show startling, disarming loving-kindness to others.[6] God proclaimed this sort of love to be central to who He is when He showed Moses His glory. Descending in a cloud, He passed before Moses, saying:

> "The LORD, the LORD, a God merciful and gracious, slow to anger, and abounding in steadfast love [*ḥesed*] and faithfulness, keeping steadfast love [*ḥesed*] for thousands, forgiving iniquity and transgression and sin, but who will by no means clear the guilty, visiting the iniquity of the fathers on the children and the children's children, to the third and the fourth generation." (Exod. 34:6–7)

This sort of love exceeds anything we can ask or imagine. It saves sinners from themselves (see Pss. 103:1–14; 130:3–4, 7–8). It lasts forever (see 1 Chron. 16:34; Ps. 136). It is the kind of love God pledged to show Naomi's descendants throughout all time (see 2 Sam. 7:11–16).

Secondly, the fact that just these two events—the famine's end and Ruth's conception—are attributed directly to God emphasizes that He often acts indirectly. In Ruth, God accomplishes His *ḥesed* through His people's *ḥesed*. The steadfast love and kindness of Naomi, Ruth, and Boaz for each other animate the story. Each knew that life was not all about them. So even in the depths of her own grief and hopelessness, Naomi was concerned for her daughters-in-law, urging them to return to their mothers' households

---

5   4:15, NLT. The Hebrew adjective *ṭôb*, translated as "better" by the NLT, carries overtones of pleasantness. Israelites considered a family of seven sons to be ideal (see 1 Sam. 2:5).

6   Daniel I. Block writes: "*Ḥesed* is . . . a strong relational term that wraps up in itself an entire cluster of concepts, all the positive attributes of God—love, mercy, grace, kindness, goodness, benevolence, loyalty, covenant faithfulness; in short, *that quality that moves a person to act for the benefit of another without respect to the advantage it might bring to the one who expresses it*" (*Judges, Ruth,* New American Commentary 6 [Nashville: B & H, 1999], 605, my emphasis).

The little dot under the *h* with a transliterated Hebrew word means the consonant is pronounced as the *ch* in *Bach*. So *ḥesed* is pronounced *che-SED*.

because she felt it would be better for them (see 1:8–13, 15).[7] Ruth's loyal and loving reply exemplified her *ḥesed*:

> "Don't ask me to leave you and turn back. Wherever you go, I will go; wherever you live, I will live. Your people will be my people, and your God will be my God. Wherever you die, I will die, and there I will be buried. May the LORD punish me severely if I allow anything but death to separate us!" (1:16-17, NLT)

And from the very start, Boaz was kind to Ruth as part of his being loyal, kind, and loving to his kinswoman Naomi (see 2:1, 5–6, 5–16, 20). The story never portrays these saints as praying for themselves; those who practice *ḥesed* think more of others than they think of themselves.

Practicing *ḥesed* outstrips anything we can reasonably require of others. Those who don't practice it—such as when Naomi's unnamed relative decides not to redeem her field because he would endanger his inheritance by having to marry Ruth (see Ruth 4:1–6)—are doing nothing wrong. Those who do practice it are doing something extraordinary and unexpected.

Yet, startlingly (and paradoxically), God does require *ḥesed* of His people: "He has told you, O [mortal], what is good; and what does the LORD require of you but to do justice, and to love kindness [*ḥesed*], and to walk humbly with your God?" (Micah 6:8). In the New Testament, this is the love that is patient and kind, that doesn't envy or boast, that isn't arrogant or rude, that doesn't insist on its own way, that isn't irritable or resentful, and that doesn't rejoice at wrongdoing but rejoices in the truth. This kind of love bears all things, believes all things, hopes all things, and endures all things (see 1 Cor. 13:4–7).

From the moment I realized I was paralyzed, I began feeling God's steadfast love for me. Yet it still strikes me as extraordinary how, when I went to college fifteen months later, He accomplished His *ḥesed* through others' *ḥesed*. From the day I arrived as part of Seattle Pacific's class of 1972, some students, faculty, and administrators showed me startling and disarming lovingkindness—fetching my meals when I was too weak to walk to the dining hall, excusing my absences from classes while encouraging me to do everything I could to attend, and becoming my advocates and friends.

Four men in particular showed that they knew their lives were not to

---

7 Naomi implied that Orpah and Ruth had shown her *ḥesed* at 1:8—"May the LORD deal kindly [*ḥesed*] with you, as you have dealt with the dead and with me."

be all about them: David McKenna, Seattle Pacific's new President; Frank Kline, the Dean of Religion; Cliff McCrath, the Dean of Students who came to Seattle Pacific in my junior year; and Donald McNichols, a professor of English. The first three devoted scores of hours to encouraging me, enabling me to understand myself and others, and helping me find my career track. Professor McNichols spent many hours helping me improve my prose.

Practicing *hesed* is costly, often requiring a long-term commitment to another's good. God's *hesed* to me, conveyed through the *hesed* of these men, still prompts me to practice *hesed*. This often means meeting regularly with someone for months or years. When this gets tiring, I remember these men and realize how ungrateful I would be not to show to others the same sort of steadfast love God moved them to show me. When it is late in the day and I am eager to go home and yet another student wants to talk, I remember waiting to see Frank Kline. Often I had no appointment, and so I would wait until his appointments were over. Then, as I would walk into his office, he would call his wife and say, "Betty, Mark is here. I'll be late for dinner."

Discovering My Life's Meaning

My walking prompted these men to notice me. I am reminded how unnatural it looks when small children stop and stare as I walk by. Yet the visible marks of God's severe mercies to us can help us find our life's meaning.

I remember falling as I got off the bus at Seattle Pacific's Camp Casey for freshman orientation. It was embarrassing. I spent most of my time alone that weekend because I was too weak to participate in most of the activities. Yet my struggles to live a fairly normal life and stay on my feet encouraged some of my new classmates to seek me out when they were struggling. Sometimes trying to hide our struggles is inappropriate.

I learned during those years that focusing on helping others to understand and cope with their suffering gave meaning to my own suffering. God's providence in my fall became clearer. His *hesed* to me came into focus through my *hesed* to others. My life's story began to make sense. In helping others I discovered much of what has become my life's meaning—and I thus found that God was redeeming my own suffering.

Something similar happens when we are willing to help others in the light of struggles and scars they do not see. Some years ago I went through something I just couldn't understand. It felt as if God was being deliberately cruel to me. A few years later I found myself needing to help a couple whose son had committed suicide. And suddenly the reason for my own suffering became clear: As difficult as my experience had been, it gave me insights I needed in order to help them.

Paul enunciated this principle at the beginning of 2 Corinthians, when he spoke of some terrible burden—some dreadful crisis or affliction—that had so overwhelmed him and his co-worker Timothy while they were in Asia that they thought they would die (see 1:8). "But that," Paul explained, "was to make us rely not on ourselves but on God who raises the dead" (1:9). God then rescued them, teaching them to trust that he would deliver them no matter what. With their hope restored, they could encourage the Corinthians to be hopeful whenever they were suffering, no matter how difficult it might be (see 1:8–10). Paul wrote:

> Blessed be the God and Father of our Lord Jesus Christ, the Father of mercies and God of all comfort, who comforts us in all our affliction, so that we may be able to comfort those who are in any affliction, with the comfort with which we ourselves are comforted by God. . . . If we are afflicted, it is for your comfort and salvation; and if we are comforted, it is for your comfort, which you experience when you patiently endure the same sufferings that we suffer. (2 Cor. 1:3–4, 6)

The Greek terms that the ESV translates as "comfort" in these verses are better translated as *encouragement* and *encourage*, rendering the passage like this:

> Blessed be the God and Father of our Lord Jesus Christ, the Father of mercies and God of all encouragement, who encourages us in all our troubles, so that we may be able to encourage those experiencing any trouble with the encouragement with which we ourselves are encouraged by God. . . . If we are distressed, it is for your encouragement and salvation; if we are encouraged, it is for your encouragement that you experience in your patient endurance of the same sufferings that we also suffer.[8]

---

8   This is Robert H. Mounce and William D. Mounce's translation in their *The Mounce Reverse-Interlinear New Testament* (Grand Rapids: Zondervan, 2006). The Greek noun that the ESV translates as "comfort" in verse 3 is *paraklēseōs*. In verse 4, the equivalent verb is *parakalōn*. Louw & Nida say these words mean "to cause someone to be encouraged or consoled, either by verbal or non-verbal means" (Johannes P. Louw and Eugene A. Nida, eds., *Greek-English Lexicon of the New Testament* [New York: United Bible Societies, 1988, 1989], entry 25.150, vol. 1, p. 306). *Paraklēseōs* and *parakalōn* are sometimes rendered as

"Encourage" is better than "comfort" because someone can comfort us merely by patting our hand and saying, "There, there!" But Paul was not just soothing the Corinthians. He told them how God had rescued him and Timothy from a humanly hopeless situation so that the Corinthians could take courage in knowing that God was not merely *capable* of delivering His people from suffering but that He *would* deliver them.

Paul found the deeper meaning of his profound suffering in its meaning for the Corinthians: "If we are distressed, *it is for your encouragement and salvation*" (1:6a, Mounce).[9] The larger purpose of his suffering was to benefit other Christians. In fact, Paul *blessed* God for his suffering because it enabled him to help others! "Blessed be the God and Father of our Lord Jesus Christ, ... who encourages us in all our troubles, *so that* we may be able to encourage those experiencing any trouble" (1:3–4, Mounce). Paul took God's ultimate aim in encouraging him to be what it would do for others rather than what it did for him: "if we are encouraged, *it is for your encouragement*" (1:6b, Mounce). His suffering in Asia was redeemed by how he could use what he had learned through it to help other Christians.

Paul found that the encouragement he and Timothy experienced enabled them "to encourage those experiencing *any* trouble." When we are suffering deeply for the first time we often feel that no one else has ever suffered as much. Yet my experience is that profound suffering is simply profound suffering. It doesn't matter much what has caused it; once we have suffered profoundly, we know what profound suffering is—and so we can encourage those who are suffering profoundly, no matter what the cause.

Nor, paradoxically enough, do we always have to experience God's deliverance before we can begin encouraging others. I often sense God's sustaining mercy to me as I am assuring others that God has not abandoned them.

When we or our loved ones are suffering our first reaction is often to ask,

---

exhortation and *exhort* rather than *encouragement* and *encourage*, which highlights their verbal aspect. Compare the ESV with the NIV and the NLT at, e.g., Acts 11:23; Romans 12:8; 1 Thessalonians 3:2; Hebrews 3:13 and 12:5; and 1 Peter 5:12.

9   Paul and Timothy experienced what I call "profound suffering," which is suffering that is so deep and disruptive that it dominates our consciousness and at least threatens to overwhelm us, sometimes tempting us to lose all hope that our lives can ever be good again. Both acute calamities (such as losing a child to suicide) and chronic conditions (such as the day-by-day care of a severely disabled child or someone's seemingly never-ending struggle with some psychological affliction) can produce profound suffering. Whether someone experiences something as profound suffering depends in part on the person and the circumstances. I have never felt my paralysis to be profound suffering, but I have had other experiences that have been.

Why me? or Why us? We want an answer focused on ourselves. There may be such an answer. Perhaps we are suffering because of some character flaw or because we have done something wrong. I walk as I do at least in part because I wouldn't heed my father's advice not to play on such a dangerous rope swing. Sometimes we can see that our suffering is good for us, prompting us to re-examine our values or come back to Christ. Yet our quest for a personal answer may hide the fact that our lives are not to be all about us. As Paul wrote elsewhere, we should not be self-centered. We should value others more than ourselves, "not looking to [our] own interests but each of [us] to the interests of the others" (Phil. 2:4, NIV). He continued:

In your relationships with one another, have the same mindset as Christ Jesus:

Who, being in very nature God,
did not consider equality with God
something to be used to his own advantage;
rather, he made himself nothing
by taking the very nature of a servant,
being made in human likeness.
And being found in appearance as a man,
he humbled himself
by becoming obedient to death —
even death on a cross! (Phil 2:6–8, NIV)

Our Lord's mindset was the ultimate expression of *ḥesed*. In a way and to a degree that no other human being will ever exemplify, He modeled what it means to be more concerned for others than for ourselves (see Phil. 2:3, 6 with Matt. 26:36-44). And yet we are to emulate this.

Scripture asserts that God honors those who practice *ḥesed* and repays their kindness to others with kindness to them.[10] Much of the kindness we can show to others involves our encouraging them to endure when they are suffering. Practicing *ḥesed* when we are suffering is a pathway to discovering the redemption of our suffering. It can even be a pathway to finding our life's meaning.

---

10   This principle generally holds even during our earthly lifetimes, although God has not promised it will hold in this life. For the general principle, see 2 Samuel 22:26 (the word the ESV translates as "merciful" in this verse is the adjectival form of *ḥesed*) and Proverbs 19:17. For its ultimate eschatological fulfillment, see Matthew 5:7; 10:42; 25:31–46; and Luke 6:37–38.

A careful reading of the book of Ruth makes clear that God providentially made Naomi's selfless, steadfast love for Ruth the vehicle for her own restoration. When suffering overwhelms us, we may at first be unable to consider anything other than ourselves. But if I could give only one bit of advice to those who are suffering—and especially to those who are suffering profoundly—it would be this: As soon as you can, stop thinking primarily in terms of yourselves. Stop asking, "Why has God allowed this to happen to me?" Instead, be alert to those you can encourage because of how you are suffering, remembering that it is often only as we focus on relieving others' suffering that we ourselves find significant relief.[11]

The Stories of Our Lives

The award-winning novelist Reynolds Price writes:

> A need to tell and hear stories is essential to the species *homo sapiens*— second in necessity apparently after nourishment and before love and shelter. Millions survive without love or home, almost none in silence; the opposite of silence leads quickly to narrative, and *the sound of story is the dominant sound of our lives*, from the small accounts of our days' events to the vast incommunicable constructs of psychopaths.[12]

We make sense of our lives in terms of the stories we tell about them. When sufferers ask, "Why?" they are really asking for a story that explains their suffering. Sometimes, like Paul and Timothy, we know why quite quickly, and so can tell a story about what our suffering means almost immediately. Sometimes, as with my accident, we only understand the story over a significant length of time. Sometimes learning the story may take a lifetime or more.

Consider Joseph. In Genesis 37–50, we read that because he was favored by his father, he said things that led his brothers to hate him. They plotted to

---

11   As a friend of mine said after reading this section, Christian suffering is communal in nature. "God has in mind *all* of His people as He sovereignly ordains each individual's events. He has in mind all of the interactions of every saint with every other saint, and their individual physical, psychological, and spiritual needs, and He orchestrates their experiences *and their sharing of those experiences* to sanctify the church."

12   Reynolds Price, *A Palpable God: Thirty Stories Translated from the Bible with An Essay on the Origins and Life of Narrative* (Berkeley, CA: North Point, 1985), 3; my emphasis.

kill him but then sold him into slavery instead. Taken to Egypt, he rose, by God's blessing, to oversee everything Pharaoh's captain of the guard owned. But Potiphar's wife wanted him, and when he wouldn't sleep with her, she accused him of the very act he had rejected because it would have betrayed his master and been a sin.

Believing his wife, Potiphar threw Joseph into prison. God gave him favor with the warden, who put him in charge of everything. Sometime later, Pharaoh threw his cupbearer and baker into prison. One night they both had dreams. Joseph interpreted their dreams, predicting that in three days the cupbearer would regain his position and the baker would be put to death. He asked the cupbearer to remember him when he regained his position. But although everything happened as Joseph said, the cupbearer forgot Joseph, leaving him in prison.

Two years later, Pharaoh had two dreams that his wise men and magicians couldn't interpret. Then the cupbearer told Pharaoh about Joseph, and so Pharaoh sent for him. Joseph told Pharaoh his dreams meant that God was sending seven years of great abundance and then seven years of severe famine to the region, so Pharaoh should appoint a wise, discerning man to supervise the stockpiling of food during the good years so that Egypt could survive the bad ones. Pharaoh recognized God's Spirit in Joseph and so appointed him, making him his second-in-command. He also made Joseph part of Egyptian royalty by giving him an Egyptian name and a prominent Egyptian bride.

Joseph's wife bore him two sons. He called the first Manasseh, which means "causing to forget," saying, "It is because God has made me forget all my trouble and all my father's household." He called the second Ephraim, which means "making doubly fruitful," saying, "It is because God has made me fruitful in the land of my suffering" (Gen. 41:51–52, NIV). These names show Joseph identified with his new family and his new life, recognizing some of the good God had brought through his suffering. But so far he knew nothing about its deeper meaning.

The famine began, and in due course Jacob sent Joseph's brothers to Egypt to buy food. When they appeared before him, he recognized them but they didn't recognize him. Deciding to test them, he accused them of being spies and, when they told him they had another brother, he demanded they go home and bring him back with them. After some delay, they brought Benjamin to Joseph. Wanting to be sure they were truly repentant about having sold him into slavery, Joseph honored them with a feast and then sent them on their way back home, having hatched a plot to make Benjamin his slave. When the plot was realized, their repentance became clearer, and so he told them who he was.[13] Now Joseph knew more of what his suffering was for. As he said to his brothers:

"I am your brother Joseph, the one you sold into Egypt! And now, do not be distressed and do not be angry with yourselves for selling me here, because *it was to save lives that God sent me ahead of you*. For two years now there has been famine in the land, and for the next five years there will be no plowing and reaping. But *God sent me ahead of you to preserve for you a remnant on earth and to save your lives by a great deliverance*. (Gen. 45:4–7, NIV)

It was now clear that what had happened to Joseph was not all about him. It was also about his birth family.

In fact, Joseph's suffering was part of a much larger story extending far beyond God's caring for Jacob's immediate family. As God said to Jacob when he was on his way to be reunited with his long-lost son, "Do not be afraid to go down to Egypt, for there I will make your family into a great nation. I will go with you down to Egypt, and I will bring you back again" (Gen. 46:3–4, NLT). What God did for Jacob's family was just one early step on the way God went about fulfilling His promise to Abraham to make his descendants a great nation (see Gen. 15:13-16). At the end of his story Joseph summarized what God had been doing all along. His brothers had intended to harm him by selling him into slavery, but God had intended their evil act to produce a greater good—namely, the saving of many lives, including those of many Egyptians (see Gen. 50:20). Joseph's suffering had a purpose beyond saving his birth family. But this became clear to Joseph only over a span of thirty-nine years![14]

---

13 During their first appearance before Joseph, the brothers had made statements in Hebrew that Joseph had understood, although they didn't know it. Those statements acknowledged their guilt in selling Joseph into slavery and expressed their regret (see Gen. 42:18–24). Joseph's plot to make Benjamin a slave revealed their hearts even more clearly and thus convinced Joseph that they had changed.

14 Joseph was seventeen when he was sold into slavery (see Gen. 37:2). He became Pharaoh's second-in-command at thirty (see 41:46) and then eight years later his brothers came to Egypt to buy grain (see 41:53-54). So it took twenty-one years for Joseph to realize that part of the meaning of his suffering was that God would save his family through it. When Jacob came to live in Egypt he was 130 (see 47:9) and he lived another seventeen years (see 47:28). Assuming that only two years had elapsed from the start of the famine and Jacob's arrival in Egypt (see 45:6), this adds up to thirty-nine years.

Misbegotten Stories

Stories like Joseph's settle our minds. They make sense of what has been happening to us. But they also tempt us. When something bad happens, we naturally ask, "Why?" We want a story that explains why we are suffering. But we also want to know what will happen next. What can we now expect? How will our story end? In trying to answer that question, we don't even require a happy ending. In fact, our need for closure is often so strong that we accept whatever strikes us as the most plausible story, even if it has a bad ending.

For instance, as depressed, grief-stricken Naomi arrived back in Bethlehem, she felt sure her life would never be pleasant again. Likewise Job, in the throes of his affliction, was sure his eye would "never again see good" (Job 7:7). Yet Naomi's story took a permanently pleasant turn when she laid her grandson Obed on her lap, and Job's story closes with him comfortably at home again, with the Lord blessing his "latter days . . . more than his beginning" (Job 42:12).

Job's case is instructive, furnishing a lesson and even a warning to us. Both he and his friends were eager to explain his suffering. They thought the story had to be that Job was an egregious, secret sinner whom God was finally exposing. Job thought the story was that God had wronged him (see Job 19:6). So he sought an audience with God where he could press his case. When he finally got one, God manifested His displeasure by appearing in a whirlwind. He then challenged Job: "Who is this that questions my wisdom with such ignorant words? Brace yourself like a man, because I have some questions for you, and you must answer them" (38:2–3, NLT). Job thought he understood God's ways (see 38:4–5). He thought he was seeing everything more or less whole, when in fact his knowledge even of his own story was crucially incomplete. *We* know that Job's miseries were occasioned by God's great regard for his righteousness and that his suffering was meant to prove that his exemplary fear of God would survive the removal of all of the benefits that had accompanied it (see 1:8–12; 2:3–6). But *Job* didn't know he was being tested, and if he had, there would have been no test.

God's first set of questions was meant to make Job realize he couldn't fathom God's wisdom. They succeeded and Job declared, "I am nothing— how could I ever find the answers? I will cover my mouth with my hand. I have said too much already. I have nothing more to say" (40:4–5, NLT). But God persisted: "Would you discredit my justice? Would you condemn me to justify yourself?" (40:8, NIV). Job was "a blameless and upright man" (2:3; see 1:1, 8) and so it wasn't wrong for him to insist on his innocence. But it seems he thought he could appear regally before God and successfully contend against him (see 31:35–37). And so God challenged Job's assumption that he controlled his fate:

> Have you an arm like God,
>   and can you thunder with a voice like his?
> Adorn yourself with majesty and dignity;
>   clothe yourself with glory and splendor.
> Pour out the overflowings of your anger,
>   and look on everyone who is proud and abase him.
> Look on everyone who is proud and bring him low
>   and tread down the wicked where they stand.
> Hide them all in the dust together;
>   bind their faces in the world below.
> *Then will I also acknowledge to you*
>   *that your own right hand can save you.* (40:9–14)

Only God can do these things. He alone is Lord of history. Lacking God's power, majesty, dignity, glory, and splendor, Job couldn't force God to vindicate him. If he were to receive justice, then God would have to give it.

God's speeches to Job stressed He is both Creator and Lord (see chaps. 38–40). Consequently, His perspective on things is vastly different than ours, at once perfectly detailed and comprehensively panoramic. As the world's Maker and Sustainer, only He fully knows and completely rules over the natural and moral worlds. He alone knows the story of the world's beginning, middle, and end (see Isa. 46:9b–11; Matt. 24:36).

At the end of God's speeches, Job finally understood:

> "I know that you can do all things;
>   no purpose of yours can be thwarted. . . .
>   Surely I spoke of things I did not understand,
>   things too wonderful for me to know. . . .
> My ears had heard of you
>   but now my eyes have seen you.
> Therefore I despise myself
>   and repent in dust and ashes." (42:2–3, 5–6, NIV)

Job's despair had arisen because he had embraced a misbegotten story, one that lacked crucial information and settled too quickly on an explanation of his suffering. He had thought he could only make sense of his story by concluding God was unfair. Wasn't there reason to hope his righteousness would ultimately be rewarded?[15] There was, but he had been expecting his rewards too soon.

Living By Faith

The antidote to the despair that comes from embracing a misbegotten story is to live by faith. Hebrews 11 shows us what that means. Living by faith means believing God—in other words, believing what God says and living according to it—even about things that are yet unseen (see vv. 1, 7).

Believing God is not the same as believing a likely story. Many of the Old Testament saints commended in Hebrews 11 couldn't tell likely stories about how their lives would end. "It was by faith," we are told, "that Abraham obeyed when God called him to leave home and go to another land that God would give him as his inheritance. *He went without knowing where he was going*" (v. 8, NLT). When he got there, he had to continue living by faith—for while he was living in the land God had promised to him, "he was like a foreigner, living in tents" (v. 9, NLT). At some point he came to realize God was not giving him just a piece of earth. Faith enabled him, as well as Isaac and Jacob, to welcome their inheritance from afar, acknowledging they would never be more than "foreigners and nomads here on earth" (v. 13, NLT). By faith, "they were longing for a better country—*a heavenly one*," and therefore "God is not ashamed to be called their God" (v. 16, NIV).

By faith Abraham believed when God promised him a son, although he had become impotent and his wife, Sarah, was both barren and past child-bearing age.[16] Isaac's birth was humanly inconceivable. And yet because

---

15   For evidence that Job practiced *ḥesed*, see 29:11–17. For his expectations stemming from that, see 29:18–20 and especially 31:3—"Is not calamity for the unrighteous, and disaster for the workers of iniquity?"

16   We find this in Hebrews 11:

> By faith Sarah herself *received power to conceive*, *even when she was past the age*, since she considered him faithful who had promised. Therefore from one man, *and him as good as dead*, were born descendants as many as the stars of heaven and as many as the innumerable grains of sand by the seashore. (vv. 11–12)

Genesis 17 clarifies how humanly hopeless Abraham took the situation to be, for when God reiterated to him that he was to have a son by Sarah, we are told he "fell on his face and laughed and said to himself, 'Shall a child be born to a man who is a hundred years old? Shall

Abraham and Sarah believed the One "who brings the dead back to life and who creates new things out of nothing" (Rom. 4:17, NLT), they hoped in spite of complete human hopelessness—and so their descendants have become as numerous as the stars in the heavens and the grains of sand by the sea (see Gen. 22:16–17; Rom. 4:16–21; and Heb. 11:12).

Some of those commended in Hebrews 11 did great things through faith, conquering kingdoms, securing justice, obtaining promises, stopping lions' mouths, walking in the midst of flames, escaping the edge of the sword, having their weakness turned to strength, and putting whole armies to flight (see vv. 33–34). Some women saw loved ones resurrected (see v. 35). Yet others were tortured, refusing to accept release "so that they might gain an even better resurrection." Some faced jeering, bloody floggings, "and even chains and imprisonment" (vv. 35-36, NIV). Some were stoned to death; others sawed in two; some were cut down by sword. Some were dressed in rags, wandering about "in deserts and mountains, living in caves and in holes in the ground" (vv. 37-38, NIV).

Yet no matter what their earthly story and whatever they did or didn't receive, all of these Old Testament saints kept the faith. Because they believed God, they lived in the light of things yet unseen, trusting He would ultimately fulfill His promises.

We Must Expect to Suffer

Hebrews 11 was written to encourage us to persevere in our faith. God promises us, as he promised Abraham, Isaac, Jacob, and the first-century Christians to whom the book of Hebrews was written, an everlasting inheritance, but only if we, as they, continue living by faith (see Heb. 3:7–4:11; 1 Cor. 15:1–2). Believing God about what we cannot yet see is especially crucial for us when we are suffering.

We need to live by faith because in this world we will have trouble (see John 16:33). Our Lord knew some of us would face hunger, thirst, estrangement, sickness, poverty, and imprisonment.[17] He said some of us will be

---

Sarah, who is ninety years old, bear a child?'" (v. 17). Even in her prime childbearing years, Sarah had not been able to bear a child. So Abraham said to God, "Oh that Ishmael"—his now-teenaged son by Sarah's servant Hagar—"might live before you!" (v. 18). The only plausible story Abraham could imagine involved Ishmael being his promised heir.

17   Jesus declared that part of the evidence that will be cited at the Final Judgment in order to separate His true followers from others will be whether someone cared for his

prosecuted and dragged before political leaders to defend our faith, and some of our families will hate us, handing us over for execution (see Matt. 10:16-21). He declared we will be hated by everyone because of him, which will cause the love of many professed believers to grow cold, yet if we endure "to the end [we] will be saved" (see Matt. 10:22 and 24:9–13).

The rest of the New Testament reiterates this. After commending those who lived by faith in Hebrews 11, Hebrews 12 encourages us to "run with endurance the race . . . set before us," remembering what Jesus endured so that we don't grow weary and give up (see vv. 1–3). We are urged not to forget Proverbs' exhortation that "addresses [us] as a father addresses his son"; saying,

> "My son, do not make light of the Lord's discipline,
> and do not lose heart when he rebukes you,
> because the Lord disciplines the one he loves,
> and he chastens everyone he accepts as his son."
> (Heb. 12:5-6, NIV, quoting Prov. 3:11–12).

Undergoing this discipline is painful (see v. 11)—in other words, it involves suffering—but it shows that God is treating us as His children. And later it will produce "a harvest of righteousness and peace for those who have been trained by it" (v. 11, NIV; see vv. 7–10).

Paul told the Corinthians that their sharing in his sufferings meant they would also share in God's comfort (see 2 Cor. 1:7). Later, in Romans, he wrote, "Now we call [God], 'Abba, Father.' For his Spirit joins with our spirit to affirm that we are God's [true] children. And since we are his children, we are his heirs. In fact, together with Christ we are heirs of God's glory. But *if we are to share his glory, we must also share his suffering*" (Rom. 8:16–17, NLT).

Because he was our Lord's specially chosen instrument for carrying Jesus' name to the whole world, Paul was destined to suffer enormously (see Acts 9:15–16). He chronicled some of his suffering in 2 Corinthians. In addition to his life-despairing experience in Asia, he endured three shipwrecks (not including the one mentioned in Acts), with one involving a night and a day

---

Christian brothers and sisters when they were hungry or thirsty or lonely or sick or naked or imprisoned (see Matt. 25:31–46). But this could not serve as evidence if no Christians suffer in these ways.

Matthew 25:31–46 is often read as requiring Christians to minister to everyone, including non-Christians. For what I take to be the correct interpretation, see D. A. Carson, *The Expositor's Bible Commentary*, vol. 8 (Grand Rapids: Zondervan, 1984), 518–23.

adrift on the open sea. He was imprisoned, repeatedly whipped as well as beaten with rods, and once stoned and left for dead. He was in danger from raging rivers and roadway robbers as well as from Jews and Gentiles and false Christians. He faced death again and again. He knew many cold and sleepless nights and hungry and thirsty days. And on top of it all, he was constantly anxious for all of the churches (see 2 Cor. 11:16–12:10).[18] Yet precisely because of what he had learned through all this, he could confidently declare, "If God is for us, who can be against us?" For how will He "who did not spare his own Son but gave him up for us all, . . . not also with him graciously give us all things?" (Rom. 8:31–32).

How Our Stories Will End

Paul had learned through his suffering to trust God and His promises, for in his suffering he had experienced God's love and deliverance again and again. Regarding the life-despairing experience he and Timothy had in Asia, he said: "He delivered us from such a deadly peril, and he will deliver us. *On him we have set our hope that he will deliver us again*" (2 Cor. 1:10). Elsewhere in his epistles, he invoked this hope repeatedly.[19] Firmly convinced of our Lord's resurrection and our reconciliation with God through Him, he proclaimed: "For I am sure that neither death nor life, nor angels nor rulers, nor things present nor things to come, nor powers, nor height nor depth, nor anything else in all creation, will be able to separate us from the love of God in Christ Jesus our Lord" (Rom. 8:38). Trusting in this truth is the hope that accompanies saving faith (see Rom. 8:24).[20]

---

18   Paul Barnett explores in detail the place of suffering in Paul's life and ministry in his *2 Corinthians* (Grand Rapids: Eerdmans, 1997).

19   See Romans 5:3-5; 8:20-25; 12:12; 15:4; and 15:13, where he calls God "the God of hope" and invokes "the power of the Holy Spirit" to help us "abound in hope." In addition, see Ephesians 1:18; Colossians 1:23, 27; 1 Thessalonians 1:3; 5:8; 2 Thessalonians 2:16; and Titus 1:2 and 3:7. Hope is also a major theme in Hebrews (see, e.g., 3:6; 6:11, 18–19; 10:23) and in 1 Peter, where we find the same invocation of faith and hope in response to suffering as we find in Paul and in Hebrews (see 1 Peter 1:3-7; 4:13).

20   Douglas J. Moo comments on this verse: "Christians, though saved, are nevertheless also saved 'with hope' — and hope, by its very nature, means that expectant and patient waiting is going to be necessary. . . . Always our salvation, while definitively secured for us at conversion, has had an element of incompleteness, in which the forward look is necessary. . . . "hope" . . . involves looking in confidence for that which one cannot see" (*The Epistle to the Romans* [Grand Rapids: Eerdmans, 1996], 521–22).

But we must not pin our hope on whether we are able to tell a plausibly detailed story about how God will keep us in His love. Paul could not always tell such stories. He could be *troubled* in many ways, *perplexed* about his circumstances and how God would work good for him in them, *hounded* by enemies, and even *floored* by what was happening to him. In other words, even he was subject to all sorts of unpleasant and potentially disorienting mental states. Yet he declared that though he was troubled, he was not *completely overwhelmed*; though he was perplexed, his perplexity did not *drive him to despair*; though he was hounded by those who hated him, he was not *forsaken*; and though he was floored by what was happening to him, he was not *destroyed*. [21] He continued hoping even in humanly hopeless circumstances.

How could he? The answer has several parts. First, he had learned through personal experience that something may feel differently than how it actually is. This taught him endurance and developed his character so that he could hope steadily (see Rom. 5:3–5). Second, he knew from Scripture that a life of faith must also be a life of hope, expecting God's final and complete fulfillment of His promises only in the *eschaton*.[22] Third, he had learned to lift his eyes from his suffering to anticipate what he could not yet see, reminding himself, as he reminds us, that whatever we are going through, no matter how awful, is but a *"light momentary affliction"* that *"is preparing us for an eternal weight of glory beyond all comparison,* as we look not to the things that are seen but to the things that are unseen. For the things that are seen are transient, but the things that are unseen are eternal" (2 Cor. 4:17–18). Thus armed, Paul could continue hoping even when he could not tell a plausible

---

Paul goes on to say that "hope that is seen is not hope. For who hopes for what he sees? But if we hope for what we do not see, we wait for it with patience" (8:24b–25). The word the ESV translates as *patience* (*hupomonē* in Greek) and Moo translates as *endurance* or *patient endurance* "suggests," according to Moo, "the connotation of 'bearing up' under intense pressure" (522), including no doubt the intense pressure of profound suffering.

21 See 2 Corinthians 4:8–9. The first four italicized terms in my text all, in this passage, express mental states, while the latter four express what Paul knows to be objectively the case. The translations are my own.

22 See Romans 15:4, 2 Timothy 3:14–17, and, again, Hebrews 11. I use the word *eschaton* to refer to the time after our Lord returns to wrap up this world's history. That time, also known as the Consummation, will inaugurate a new heaven and a new earth, where His saints "will be his people, and God himself will be with them as their God. He will wipe away every tear from their eyes, and death shall be no more, neither shall there be mourning, nor crying, nor pain anymore, for the former things have passed away" (Rev. 21:3–4). We will then begin to marvel for all eternity at the stories of God's grace and mercy to us.

story about how God would deliver him.[23] He knew by faith that God would work everything in his life together for good (see Rom. 8:28), even though how God would do so was not something he could yet see.

And so, Paul concluded,

> we know that if the tent that is our earthly home is destroyed, we have a building from God, a house not made with hands, eternal in the heavens. . . . For while we are still in this tent, we groan, being burdened—not that we would be unclothed, but that we would be further clothed, so that what is mortal may be swallowed up by life. He who has prepared us for this very thing is God, who has given us the Spirit as a guarantee.
> *So we are always of good courage. We know that while we are at home in the body we are away from the Lord, for we walk by faith, not by sight.* (2 Cor. 5:1, 4–7)

Paul had learned that what happens to God's saints in this world is never the last word.

Broken Wholeness

In fact, that last word will be much more marvelous than anything we can now imagine it to be. For Paul's declaration at 2 Corinthians 4:16–17 means this: No matter what we suffer in this world, we will know in glory that our suffering was an integral part of an even greater good. We will then realize that if we could go back and relive our lives, we would not trade that good for less suffering.

Right now, I don't know the details about how my story will end. Sometimes I'm troubled by the ever-increasing consequences of my accident. Even this morning I find myself asking, "Will what I am experiencing today stop me from being able to teach, to speak, and to preach?" I have sometimes been deeply perplexed by what was happening to me and how God could be working in it for my good. But I know my story's Author, and I know what He has promised will be its end. I know He has often turned real evils into

---

23 Paul sometimes uses military metaphors to urge his readers to fight the good fight of faith. See, e.g., Ephesians 6:10-20, 1 Timothy 6:12, and especially 2 Thessalonians 5:8—"But since we belong to the day, let us be sober, having put on the breastplate of faith and love, *and for a helmet the hope of salvation.*"

greater goods for me. And I know it is through suffering that He prompts me to lift my gaze above the world's distractions to live in conscious dependence on Him. My suffering focuses me, driving those distractions away.

Our Lord declared, "I came that they may have life and have it abundantly" (John 10:10). My accident and all the other suffering I have known have given me a life abundant in its depth and meaning. Like Paul, "I am content with weaknesses, insults, hardships, persecutions, and calamities. For when I am weak, then I am strong" (2 Cor. 12:10). Through all such things, God has graciously broken me to teach me that I can be whole only in Him. Knowing that is abundant life indeed.

Discussion Questions

1. How has God used the *ḥesed* of others to redeem suffering in your life? What can you do to "pass on" that *ḥesed* to others who are suffering?
2. Have you ever been discouraged by looking for the purpose of your suffering within your own life? How might your perspective change when you think about the way your suffering can influence others?
3. Hebrews 11 lists a number of saints who persevered in faith through suffering. What sufferings saints, biblical or otherwise, particularly inspire you to persevere, and in what way(s)?
4. How does understanding faith as the hope of things not seen influence your response to your own suffering?

Resources for Further Study

Books

Timothy Keller, *Walking with God through Pain and Suffering* (New York: Riverhead, 2015)

John Piper and Justin Taylor, eds., *Suffering and the Sovereignty of God* (Wheaton, IL: Crossway, 2006)

Joyce Sackett. *Goodbye, Jeanine: A Mother's Faith Journey After Her Daughter's Suicide* (Colorado Springs, CO: NavPress, 2005)

Joni Eareckson Tada, *A Place of Healing: Wrestling with the Mysteries of Suffering, Pain, and God's Sovereignty* (Colorado Springs, CO: David C. Cook, 2015)

Article

Mark R. Talbot, "True Freedom: The Liberty that Scripture Portrays as Worth Having," in John Piper, Justin Taylor, and Paul Kjoss Helseth, eds., *Beyond the Bounds: Open Theism and the Undermining of Biblical Christianity* (Crossway, 2003)

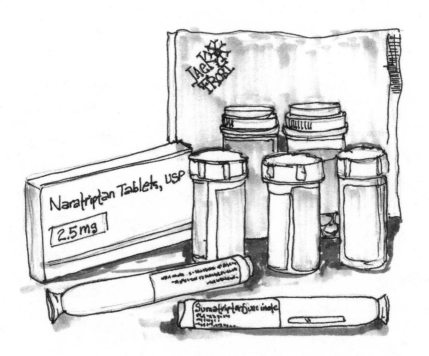

THREE

Redeeming Chronic Pain:
When Surgery Fails

MARK MCGINNISS

"Hear, and I will speak; I will question you, and you make it known to me." I had heard of you by the hearing of the ear, but now my eye sees you. (Job 42:4–5, ESV)[1]

While there is no prize for the one who can boast the greatest pain, the medical profession reports I can crow about coming in second. In the fall of 2010, I was diagnosed with trigeminal neuralgia, or TN as it is commonly called.

TN is a chronic pain condition that affects the trigeminal nerve, the fifth and largest cranial nerve. It has three branches on each side of the face: one branch follows the upper part of the face from the middle of the ear to the forehead; a second branch traces a path from the same origin along the upper jaw to the eye socket; the third branch follows the lower jaw line to the lip and lower mouth area. TN typically occurs on one side of the face; I am one of three percent of sufferers who experiences pain on both sides.[2]

TN is characterized by sudden, intense jolts of searing pain that last anywhere from a few seconds to a few minutes. Sufferers have described the pain many ways: hot knives being twisted into the face or a thunderstorm exploding on the face. To me, it feels like having one end of jumper cables

---

1 All Scripture quotations taken from the NASB.

2 Medical News Today, "What is Trigeminal Neuralgia? What Causes Trigeminal Neuralgia?" accessed April 2, 2015, http://www.medicalnewstoday.com/articles/160252.php.

hooked to a high-voltage battery and the other end connected to my face. While most pain episodes do not last long (my episodes usually last only a few seconds), they may occur in rapid succession, allowing no relief. TN comes second only to cluster headaches among the worst pains known to medical science,[3] worse even than kidney stones or labor pain (though I would not argue the point with any mother).

TN affects more women than men and usually assaults people over 50, although people of any age—even children—may be struck with this insidious disease. It is rare, affecting only twelve people per 100,000.[4] The number of patients with TN varies from 45,000[5] to 400,000 in the United States.[6] To those who endure such agony these statistics provide no comfort. This is one situation where misery does not love company.

The disease is not lethal, but it has been called the "suicide disease." People who suffer with TN have been known to take their own lives because of the intensity of their pain and science's inability to help. Having lived with this pain non-stop for more than five years with no hope of relief in sight, I understand the intense desire to stop the agony at nearly any cost.

The beginning of my journey with TN might have been comical, if it did not hurt so badly. It was a weekday morning during the spring of 2008. As I began to shave, I touched the right corner of my lip to shave my left cheek. A lightning bolt of pain exploded from the last molar on the top left side of my jaw, pain like I had never experienced before. My whole body flinched in agony. But it was over in less than a few seconds.

Not sure what had happened, I touched the left corner of my lip again. The same mind-numbing jolt repeated in exactly the same place, for exactly the same amount of time. I touched it a third time (some might be questioning my sanity at this point). Two times could be coincidence, I thought. A third trial was science. Again, intense searing pain blasted the left side of my face, its epicenter in that same molar. Since the pain seemed to be cen-

---

3 Dr. Larry Waters, editor of this book, suffers from cluster headaches. He has the dubious distinction (that I know he would rather not have) of having the worst pain known to medical science.

4 National Institute of Neurological Disorders and Stroke, "Trigeminal Neuralgia Fact Sheet," accessed April 2, 2015, http://www.ninds.nih.gov/disorders/trigeminal_neuralgia/detail_trigeminal_neuralgia.htm.

5 Ibid.

6 Trigeminal Neuralgia Association, "Frequently Asked Questions about Neuropathic Facial Pain and Trigeminal Neuralgia," accessed April 2, 2015, http://www.fpa-support.org/support/faq.html.

tered in a tooth, I contacted my dentist for an emergency appointment. My wife Joy and I were leaving the country on vacation the following weekend; I dared not travel with a bad tooth that caused such misery.

My dentist saw me the day before Joy and I were scheduled to leave town. I explained my bizarre symptoms, which I had tested two mornings before my appointment to make sure the pain was real and still present. It was very real and very present. After a thorough examination, my dentist declared that my teeth were fine, even the suspected molar. No issues whatsoever. "Then what is causing such pain?" I asked. He was not sure but suggested it might be a type of "neuralgia." I went home confused and a bit discouraged. But we had our reservations and it only hurt when I touched my face. So we decided to take the vacation, be careful not to touch my face, and pray!

On the morning of our departure, I showered and began to shave. Without thinking, I touched the corner of my lip. Realizing what I had done, I waited for the lightning bolt to strike. But there was no pain. I tentatively touched my lip again. Again, no jolts. I could not explain it, but the pain was certainly gone.

This, I later learned, is typical of TN. It attacks for a period of time and then may go into remission—but it always comes back, and with a vengeance: more intense pain, more often, and with more triggers that cause agonizing jolts. TN worsens over time without any remission.

My TN returned to stay in September 2010. Its reappearance is seared into my memory. My wife and I were to travel from northeast Pennsylvania, where we live and I teach, to Florida to conduct a weekend Bible conference on the subject of "Disappointment with God" from the book of Job. A few days before the trip, I started getting varying degrees of pain jolts not only when my face was touched, but also when I talked, drank, or ate. Eating I could give up for a weekend, but it is difficult to conduct a seminar without talking! Not sure what was happening, we decided to fulfill the commitment and check with our family doctor when we came back.

While the conference was well received, I was in misery. Every time I spoke, the pain struck. It was only by God's grace that I was able to speak four times that weekend. By Sunday, Joy was very worried, and I was in distressing pain. Questions and fears flooded our thoughts on the flight home. What was happening? My life was speaking: I am a professor and pastor. But how could I teach if I was jolted with pain every time I opened my mouth? I had spent twenty-seven years teaching God's people in a local church in New Jersey. Now God had granted my heart's desire to teach at a seminary. But all seemed to be jeopardized by a malady we could not even name—until I googled my symptoms.

While we did not want to believe the results of my research, our general practitioner confirmed my diagnosis: "Mark, you have trigeminal neuralgia." It is difficult to put into words how that one sentence has changed our lives. Since that September, not one hour has passed without some pain due to TN. Sometimes I experience more than one hundred agonizing shocks a day (yes, I have counted them, and my wife thinks I underreport). Other times I can have scores of jolts within a single minute. I do not have good days. I have bad days or awful days. The only respite a TN sufferer might enjoy is sleep.[7] While this is a mercy, it provides little help for coping with TN when awake.

Because TN pain is agonizing and unpredictable, a sufferer deals not only with the terrible physical suffering but with emotional turmoil as well. With the randomness of the jolts comes fear. "When will the pain strike?" (With TN the question is always *when,* never *if.*) "How painful will it be?" "Will I be able to handle it?" The life you once knew has been shattered like a tree hit by lightning. All that remains is a charred and unrecognizable visage of a self you once knew.

Having given us the official diagnosis, our doctor referred us to an area neurologist. There I rehearsed my nondescript medical history and current unique symptoms: whenever I touch my face, eat, speak, yawn, or even smile, I am jolted with pain. A cold wind, air conditioning, or a kiss from my wife will trigger terrible paroxysms. After speaking with me and observing the random jolts of pain as we spoke, the neurologist concurred: I did indeed have the "suicide disease," also called *tic douloureux*, a fancy French word for "painful tic." The name fits. Depending on the severity of the electrical stab, the face spasms. My family calls it a twitch. There is no hiding the jolt—it clearly shows on the sufferer's face.

---

7   One of the characteristics of the disease is that many with TN are able to sleep without being awakened by pain. This does not mean that they do not experience pain; it simply means they are not awakened—which is a divine mercy to be sure. My wife believes I still have jolts during the night, though I do not awaken. A recent study seems to corroborate her observations: "Pain paroxysms in trigeminal neuralgia (TN) are sudden and extremely intense. Nonetheless, many clinicians who treat TN report that patients are rarely if ever awakened at night by pain attacks. If true, this observation is important as it implies the presence of a powerful sleep protective mechanism. We queried TN patients and their habitual sleep partners about painful awakenings and discovered that such awakenings are in fact quite common. As during the day, pain paroxysms during sleep are typically induced by natural stimuli at TN trigger points. Brief attacks sometimes occur without frankly awakening the patient, but they appear nonetheless to be painful" (M. Devor, I. Wood, Y. Sharav, and J. M. Zakrzewska, "Trigeminal Neuralgia during Sleep," *Pain Practice* 8, no. 4 (2008): 263–68, accessed April 2, 2015, http://www.ncbi.nlm.nih.gov/pubmed/18503619). However, some with TN suffer around the clock.

The neurologist prescribed anticonvulsant medications. These prescriptions are generally off-label anti-seizure drugs to treat epilepsy. While I would have taken anything to stop the pain, our Internet research revealed there are times these medications do not work and eventually become ineffective, not to mention that each had the potential for serious side effects. There is no drug specifically designed for the treatment of TN; the most that these could do would be to help manage the pain. Although we started the prescription regimen, Joy and I desired a solution, not management.

There is only one procedure that offers a potential cure for TN, an invasive brain surgery called microvascular decompression (MVD). The working medical hypothesis is that TN occurs when a blood vessel (or more than one) compresses the trigeminal nerve exiting the brain stem to such a degree that it wears away the nerve's protective myelin lining. The offending blood vessel "compressing" the exposed nerve produces the associated pain. MVD, an approximately five-hour brain surgery, separates the trigeminal nerve from any blood vessels pressing against it. During the procedure the neurosurgeon cuts through the scalp, drills through the skull, locates the blood vessel or vessels squeezing against the trigeminal nerve, and then "decompresses" them by inserting a piece of Teflon or other artificial material between the nerve and vessels to keep the compression from returning.

With any brain surgery, potential complications and dangers abound. Our neurologist quickly pointed out the possibility of bleeding, infection, cerebral fluid leak, and of course death. He explained that the trigeminal nerve is the width of a human hair and that the surgeon would be working in an area no larger than a quarter of an inch square. While he tried his best to dissuade us from such a dangerous surgery, my wife had discovered just that morning that Johns Hopkins Hospital in Baltimore was part of our insurance plan. More importantly, they boasted a TN research center. With referral in hand and renewed hope for a cure, we headed for one of the country's premier hospitals.

As our hopes soared, so did the pain. While we waited for an appointment, fall turned to winter, and I discovered that wind, especially a cold or even chilly one (fairly common for northeast Pennsylvania), would cause severe face shocks. I began wearing a scarf, not to be fashionable, but to protect my face against the wind. But there, quite literally, is the rub. Whenever I wore the scarf, I had to be very careful that it did not come in contact with my cheek, or it would trigger the same degree of pain from which I was trying to protect myself.

Arctic blasts are not the only danger. Amplified noise also causes severe jolts. Once during a seminary chapel service, I was jarred right out of my seat with a bolt of pain. I caught myself just before I hit the floor. I experience the same pain every Sunday at our church's worship service. Such pain may bring unbidden tears but I fear wiping away the tears because touching my face would produce more pain. But if the tears are left unchecked, they could trigger pain as they cascade down my cheek. A catch-22.

While waiting for my appointment at Hopkins, I had the privilege of doing a weekend retreat for married couples at a New York church. I love speaking on marriage; the Song of Solomon is a special interest of mine. Unfortunately, my wife became sick at the last minute and could not attend with me. But TN did. Although I can try to hide the jolts and pain from others, I cannot when the pain is severe. Early in the weekend I had a particularly brutal session, and one of the participants noticed. He approached and introduced himself as a doctor. He gently asked if I was having health issues. His gentleness left when he discovered I had TN. "Oh, do you know that what you have is called the 'suicide disease'? Many TN sufferers take their own lives because they cannot handle the pain." That was all he had to offer. I thanked the doctor for his observation. As he walked away I wondered where he and my neurologist had trained for their bedside manners.

When the day of our appointment finally arrived, we were full of hopeful expectations. Not only were we at a top hospital, but our appointment was with the renowned pediatric neurosurgeon, Dr. Ben Carson.[8] Dr. Carson gained fame as the first surgeon to successfully separate twins conjoined at the head. While his busy pediatric practice counted for three-quarters of his time, the rest was dedicated to serving patients with TN. Not only is Carson a gifted surgeon, he is also a man of faith. He sought God's favor before each of his surgeries, praying over his patients in the operating room. I was certainly in good hands.

After a comprehensive and unrushed physical exam by his physician's assistant and TN veteran, Carol James, we had another lengthy exam with Dr. Carson. Both concluded that I did indeed have TN. They also told me that I did not have a "suicide disease"; advances in medical research had made TN treatable and curable. Dr. Carson believed I was a good candidate for an MVD surgery. Although I did not need to be convinced, they talked us through the pros and cons of an MVD. While the possible complications were significant, the chance of life without pain muted any side effects. This surgery boasted a 90–95% success rate of eliminating all pain. Granted, the recovery was a bit rough: a few days in an neurological intensive care unit, at least two more

---

8   Carson's autobiography is called *Gifted Hands: The Ben Carson Story*. There is also a 2009 movie about Carson with the same title.

in a regular hospital room, and four weeks convalescing at home. While the complications of the operation were formidable—a small chance of death, bleeding, infection, headache, leaking of cerebral spinal fluid—we clung to that 95%. Although TN jolts came hot and heavy as we spoke, our hearts soared on the drive home as we contemplated a future without TN.

The downside of being attended by a world-renowned physician is the wait for an opening in his schedule. My brain surgery was scheduled for Easter week, a few months away. Appropriate, I thought. As we rejoiced in Jesus conquering sin and the grave on Easter, we would celebrate being delivered from this terrible disease. Although the pain was a constant companion, so was hope. A 95% success rate and an end to this nightmare resided in the forefront of our minds and prayers.

Still, we needed to deal with the constant, agonizing torment for a few more months. My suffering did not relent. On a "bad day" I would usually have thirty pain-free minutes. On an "awful day" TN would stir me from that just-before-waking-sleep with a crushing jolt. What an alarm clock. Once the pain commenced, I had no relief for the rest of the day. The only variables would be how many times and with what intensity the jolts would strike. Would I experience ten to twenty jolts in a minute, or would there be twenty in an hour? Not an hour would pass without some explosion of pain. I was sometimes jolted so hard in class I would cry out in pain. I hated those times; they made the students uncomfortable and diverted their attention from parsing Hebrew verbs. But my students always responded sympathetically and compassionately, even if they did not know what to say or do.

Meals guaranteed increased distress. While a TN sufferer can miss a meal or two, starving oneself is not a health-positive way to deal with TN. I remember one dinner that I made it through with minimal pain. But as I cleared the table, a blow of pain hit me so hard and so quickly that it physically knocked me to my knees. I nearly dropped all the plates I carried. Such pain would continue through the evening and follow me to bed. As I lay waiting for the peace of sleep, I wished for a sleep switch I could throw that would deliver me from pain. Every night features a race to see what wins: sleep or TN. Would I fall asleep mercifully delivered from any more shocks, or would I get jolted and then fall asleep? Most times TN wins that race.

While the pain is excruciating for me, I feel it is worse for those who love me the most. Joy and I have five children. By the time I was diagnosed with TN, two of our oldest boys, Jeremy and Drew, had married fine women and were making their own homes. My third son, Ian, was starting his career as an equestrian in New Jersey. While my older sons and their families understood and sympathized with my pain, it was left to my wife and our two youngest, Kasey and Kyle, to experience the ravages of TN firsthand at home.

TN was a monster that attacked not only me but my family as well. Though forced to watch me suffer, they could do nothing to help. They could not offer medication, therapy, or even a visit to the doctor. Knowing that they were powerless made my family's emotional pain worse. As a father and husband, watching emotional turmoil in those I love the most deepened my pain. While I could hide from familial interaction and try to protect those I love by not showing pain, isolation is a poor strategy for those dealing with TN or any chronic pain. Chronic pain or illness of any sort is isolating enough in and of itself simply because others do not hurt in the same way (Ps. 13).[9] However, intentionally hiding one's self from others leaves one alone with the very monster one hates! I tried this once. My wife found me crying alone in our bedroom closet. She made me promise I would not hide the pain by sequestering myself from her. It's not an easy promise to keep when I see the sadness reflected in the eyes of those who are hurting for me while I, as the sufferer, can do nothing to take away their hurt because I can do nothing about my own pain. But I would be physically and emotionally lost without Joy's warm touch assuring me I am not alone in my pain.

Still, while we waited for surgery, God's grace sustained us both through His Spirit and the prayers of His people. From New Jersey to California, from as far south as Florida, and from across the waters in Scotland, friends interceded for us. God also provided people who reached out to us in practical ways. Since the surgery was going to be out of town, Joy needed a place to stay in Baltimore for a week. This meant additional costs: travel, parking, hotel, food, etc. In all our needs, God provided. Traveling on the fervent prayers of our brothers and sisters, being in the hands of a brilliant neurosurgeon, and having the medical statistics so much in our favor, we headed to Baltimore and Johns Hopkins with hopes of a not-too-distant-future without TN.

But even through the haze of anesthesia, I knew my surgery had failed. As I lay in intensive care attached to a tangle of tubes and wires, vaguely aware of the chirping of monitors and sundry medical equipment, I knew beyond a shadow of a doubt TN was still with me. I tried to talk myself out of the realization. I was still groggy—maybe I only dreamt the TN jolt? Didn't I vaguely remember Joy telling me that Dr. Carson was extremely pleased with the surgery? That he had discovered a compression of the trigeminal nerve and decompressed it? How could I be feeling jolts? Plus, how could I

---

9   Notice how many times David uses the first-person singular pronoun as he describes his emotional pain of feeling abandoned by God.

tell my wife and daughter, who waited by my hospital bed expecting good news, that the surgery we had set our hopes on had failed? Pain has a way of sobering one quickly. It was definitely another TN jolt I had just felt. Once I acknowledged the truth, tears flowed unbidden. Sadly, those tears would not be the last. Nor would this be the last time that our hopes, bolstered by medical statistics, would be soundly crushed in a neurological intensive care unit.

Although Easter did not bring deliverance from TN as we had hoped, I did improve slightly. The jolts remained intense, but they occurred less frequently. A day once filled with more than a hundred jolts now only held twenty or sometimes even fewer. Still, we had hoped for a complete cure. At our post-op appointment, Dr. Carson suggested a glycerol rhizotomy. He would insert a long needle through my left cheek and, with the help of x-ray, advance the needle to the base of my skull just behind my left eye, where the ganglion of the trigeminal nerve is located. Once in place he would inject liquid glycerol to destroy the pain sensors of the TN nerve. Although this was an outpatient surgery, it was done under general anesthesia. Dr. Carson was confident this procedure, while not permanent, would eliminate any remaining pain. This rhizotomy could be repeated if and when the nerves regrew and the pain returned, likely in five to seven years. The side effects were minimal and the prognosis once again was very good. With our hearts filled with renewed hope, the renewed prayers of friends, and the overwhelming statistical probability of medical success, two months later we retraced our steps to Johns Hopkins.

When I awoke from my glycerol rhizotomy, I looked like a lopsided chipmunk. The left side of my face was swollen and completely numb. Surely, I thought, such deep numbness would stop any TN pain. It did not. Though Dr. Carson said the procedure had gone well, the TN began jolting me again as soon as I regained consciousness. Once again we were on the wrong side of medical statistics. Once again our hopes were dashed.

Unfortunately, numbness and the crushing of hope were not the only side effects. The rhizotomy reversed the improvement I had experienced after the MVD. The TN pain was intense and increasing. Although Carol James increased my prescription, it had no effect. Nor was Dr. Carson able to explain exactly what had happened. He surmised that something "must be anatomically and physiologically different" with my system.[10] I was turning out to be, in their words, a "very unique case."

Although medical success had eluded us, Dr. Carson and Carol James would not give up on me as a patient. They referred me to Dr. Jeffery Brown

---

10   Five years later, I still have that phone message from Dr. Carson on my office voice mail.

in Long Island, New York, a specialist published in the area of TN treatment and research to whom Dr. Carson sent all his most difficult cases. Although I was not excited to be a "difficult" patient, we were grateful once again for a renewed sense of hope that something could be done to offer relief.

After an extensive exam with a specialized MRI, Dr. Brown discovered additional compression of my TN nerve. Dr. Brown believed a second MVD could provide the relief we so desperately sought. So we packed our bags and headed east through New York City to Long Island. Another hospital stay for me and another hotel residence for Joy. Although Dr. Brown would not provide medical percentages on our chances for a successful outcome, he was confident he could find the issue and correct it. When he met with Joy after another five-hour invasive brain surgery, he was even more confident. To say he had discovered another compression would be an understatement. My trigeminal nerve had been covered in a spider-web of veins and a large artery. He retracted the veins and separated the offending artery from the nerve. His confidence was so high that the good doctor could not quite believe when I reported to him in intensive care that I was still getting TN shocks. The surgery was a failure once again. Terrible face pain still filled our future. Although we should cognitively realize that *someone* has to be in the five to ten percent for whom procedures do not work, it is still a shock to wake up on the wrong side of statistics. The emotional difficulties are enormous. This disappointment is compounded when there are consequences to the unsuccessful surgery.

The morning I was to be discharged from the hospital, I was brushing my teeth carefully, endeavoring not to disturb my face too much. While standing over the sink with my head down, I noticed a clear liquid dripping out of my left nostril: drip, drip, drip, drip. I called for a nurse. Immediately I was in bed, surrounded with countless medical personnel. My cerebralspinal fluid (CSF), or brain fluid, was leaking through an opening in my skull out my nose. Such a situation creates an opportunity for an infection to reach the brain from the outside. It seemed that I would not die from TN but could die from the unsuccessful cure.

Dr. Brown decided to release me (and I was not arguing with him, much to the dismay of my wife) and treat the leak with medication. We were going home not only with TN but also with a life-threatening side effect. Our spirits were beyond devastated. Now the pain of TN was complicated with CSF headaches. If too much brain fluid leaks, the brain literally shifts position downward in the skull. While TN is terribly painful, CSF headaches are agonizing. My first CSF headache struck as I was walking into my bedroom one evening. Suddenly it felt like someone was splitting my skull in two. The pain consumed me. I fell on the bed sobbing, rocking back and forth in a fetal position, begging

Joy, begging God to do anything to take away the pain. Joy held me, terrified. Finally, after a few minutes of lying still on the bed, the pain began to subside. Dr. Brown determined I was too active: movement was causing my brain fluid to leak more. Thus began our "lost year." While I was able to teach, I was not permitted to do anything else. Fine with me. TN was bad enough.

After a month it was obvious that the medication was not controlling the leak or my TN. Dr. Brown decided he needed to do another surgery to address the leak. With the need for yet another brain surgery clearly evident, I asked about the wisdom of repeating the MVD. I reasoned if I was going to be in surgery we might as well go all the way and take another shot at dealing with my TN jolts. Dr. Brown agreed and scheduled me for my third MVD, which would also deal with the CSF leak.

Although past medical failures had muted our hopes, we still cried when the first jolts of TN coursed through my face as I awoke in the neurological intensive care for a third time. Not only had the surgery failed to deal with the TN, but my brain fluid continued to leak. Now we drove home through New York City traffic with another medical failure and an ongoing medical complication. It took another two surgeries with a total of five surgeons over six months back at Johns Hopkins to successfully stop the brain fluid leak. All totaled, I'd had six brain surgeries and one brain procedure (the rhizotomy) over eighteen months. The only things we had to show for such medical effort were a half-inch wide scar that begins below my ear and ends at the top left side of my scalp—and the continuing shocking jolts of TN. Most disheartening was the news that Dr. Carson and his PA, Carol James, our life rafts through this turmoil, were both retiring from medicine. While they did connect me to a neurologist, his care was less than stellar. We ended up with another potentially lethal side effect from a medication he prescribed. Without expert guidance, we suffered lost and alone.

During this time I read Tim Hansel's *You Gotta Keep Dancin': In the Midst of Life's Hurt You Can Choose Joy!* Tim lives with chronic pain after a tragic climbing accident. He writes, "All of our theology must eventually become biography."[11] Tim means that our theology—what we truly believe about God and ourselves—becomes readily apparent to ourselves and others when life crashes down, when it disappoints. It is at these times that our theology appears clearly in the warp and woof of our lives. A "good" theology writes chapters of trust in God even in the deepest pain. A "poor" theology engraves paragraphs of railing against God and what He allows in life. What

11   Tim Hansel, You *Gotta Keep Dancin': In the Midst of Life's Hurt You Can Choose Joy!* (Colorado Springs, CO: Victor, 1985), 41.

we believe about God in the midst of pain is the construction material that forms our individual lives—our biographies—which those who see us read every day. The only question is, Will their reading of us, of our living in pain, expose "good" or "poor" theology?

My days are full of painful shocks that have no pattern and no warning. The only guarantee I have is that the lightning bolts will come, and frequently. As horrible as the physical pain is and will be, the emotional pain is as terrible—maybe even worse.

Fear is part and parcel of my disease. There is fear of more pain, or of not being able to manage the pain. The ultimate fear is that the pain will become so intense and frequent that the ministry and life I know and enjoy will be lost. By God's grace we have not had to deal with this outcome as of yet—but the apprehension lurks with each episode of pain that continues longer than "normal." Thankfully, while fear reaches out its tentacles on occasion, it is not a constant companion.

An underlying sadness accompanies TN, as with any chronic medical condition. It brings sorrow over unfulfilled expectations and disappointment we did not expect at this stage of life. Joy and I had anticipated becoming empty nesters with the mixed feeling of any parents. But the lightning bolts of TN interrupt our best-laid plans and pleasures. While Joy and I can plan an intimate evening in front of the fireplace, jolts of pain quickly distract and, more times than not, kill such designs. While we adjust to the inability to enjoy certain activities, the frequent adjustment does add sadness and regret.

TN also brings the troubles of the soul—those heart sobs that sufferers vent when they are alone in the lost hours of the night. At those times the sufferer feels like Job reborn: "Why is light given to him who suffers, and life to the bitter of soul?" (Job 3:20). "I cry to You [God] for help, but You do not answer me; I stand up and You turn Your attention against me" (Job 30:20). Lewis captures the essence of the soul's problem with pain: "If God were good, he would wish to make his creatures perfectly happy, and if God were almighty, he would be able to do what he wished. But the creatures are not happy. Therefore God lacks either goodness, or power, or both."[12] As Lewis exposes, the problem as expressed (and lived) is not really a problem of pain but a problem of faith. To ask the question more crudely: Why does God allow one who loves and follows Him to experience such pain? These questions are not voiced in the clear of day or at a Sunday morning worship service. Christians, as a whole, are not comfortable around the soul-felt questions of complaint so prevalent in Job or the lament psalms. The suf-

---

12   C. S. Lewis, *Problem of Pain* (New York: HarperOne, 2001). 16.

ferer simply swallows these questions and suffers alone. But these legitimate questions have been answered in the same book that raises them.

Before I was struck with TN, when I had the opportunity to teach in other churches, at Bible conferences, and at seminars, I would always speak on Job. Since my children accompanied me on these ventures (they could probably have preached my sermons for me if something happened to me mid-presentation), they would ask why I would always speak on Job 2, "The Problem of Pain." The reason, I shared with them, is that people need the important skill of dealing well with pain. Because we live in a sin-sick world, no one gets a free pass to live this life without pain. As Shakespeare's Macduff observes:

> Each new morn
> New widows howl, new orphans cry, new sorrows
> Strike heaven on the face.[13]

Some have more pain than others. Others live through more emotional pain than physical. But no one gets from the cradle to the grave without shedding tears. So I preached Job 2 every chance I had in an effort to prepare people for pain or help them live with pain that already existed. What I did not know prior to the fall of 2010 was that while I preached to the crowds, I was actually preaching to myself. God was preparing my soul for the worst pain of my life.

While Job and others have expressed their need to know the "why" of their illnesses or pain, I have not (other than to check my life to see if TN is a function of divine discipline [see Ps. 32]; I do not believe it is). I have not asked "why" because I know the "who" of my life. When God speaks to Job out of the whirlwind, He does not answer "why." He does not explain the heavenly wager that was behind all of Job's trouble. Out of that storm, He chides Job with a series of more than seventy pointed and at times sarcastic rhetorical questions that reveal to Job who God is in all His power and wisdom (38:1–42:6). At the same time God exposes Job's inability to run the universe or even question God's own governance of it. What Job, I, and those who suffer chronic pain need the most is not an answer to the "why" but rather a renewed glimpse of God. The "who" of the whirlwind is the only answer to my storm of pain.

In his commentary on Job, Francis Anderson states, "It is easier to lower your view of God than to raise your faith to such heights."[14] When a believer encounters pain, he or she has a choice: either diminish God by stripping

---

13   Shakespeare, *Macbeth,* act 4, scene 3.
14   Francis I. Anderson, *Job,* Tyndale OT Commentary (Downers Grove, IL: Inter-Varsity Press, 2008), 93–94.

Him of His power, love, or both because He does not or will not alleviate personal suffering; or choose to trust that God is all-loving even when He will not heal and all-powerful even when He decides not to. The first option is easy; the second is not.

The last chapters of Job (38–42) clearly picture who God is and who I am. I choose daily that I would rather be defined by the "who" of my life than the "why" of my disease. So while I do not have sore boils all over my body, when I preach on Job now, I realize and stress that the book was not written to explain Job's dilemma to Job. The book was written for all those who suffer, even now.

Today my wife, Joy, came home from the dentist. She had pain, but she was not sure which tooth was causing it. The dentist needed to test each tooth in the general area. They found the tooth by making Joy feel pain. Once they thought they discovered the offending tooth through their pain test, they repeated the test three times just to make sure. Each time, Joy was more than convinced they had found the correct tooth! As Joy related her pain-filled dental trip, she asked with tears in her eyes how I get up and make it through each day.

I had no pat answer for her. Although some without pain will offer tired theological clichés, there are no easy answers for those who live with it every day. I have no strategy per se to deal with another sixteen hours of TN jolts.

But like Job, I do have God. While I do not know how He mediates it, I receive His grace daily. That grace works in me the same way it worked for the apostle Paul (2 Cor. 12:9). Grace is the power to face the day, even though barring a miracle, I will be struck with significant pain multiple times every waking hour of every day for the rest of my life. While grace does not lessen the pain, it allows me to endure it—and endure it and endure it.

As I endure by grace, I see myself living the white space within the lament psalms: that area of experiencing confidence *in* God without seeing a resolution *from* God. It is that space, for instance, in Psalm 13 where David realizes afresh that God's silence (vv. 1–2) is not to be mistaken for His absence. It is that space of affirming faith in God even though painful experience conspires against the belief that faith is well placed (vv. 5–6). This is not to say that there are no more tears. There are plenty, even after so many years of suffering with TN. Joy's shoulder is damp with them. However, I endeavor to live each day declaring with Asaph, "My flesh and my heart may fail, but God is the strength of my heart and my portion forever" (Ps. 73:26). It is my faith in God that gets me out of bed each morning knowing full well that unimaginable pain will be my lot until I lay myself down to sleep once again.

Discussion Questions

1. If you were to be subjected to Job-like suffering and someone were to write a biography of your response, how would it read? What would be the title of your story?
2. What is more important to you, knowing the "why" of your suffering or the "who" of life? Why?
3. When you are suffering, how do you view God? Do you understand God as an all-loving and all-powerful heavenly Father even when He does not end your suffering? Or do you lower your view of God, to account for His apparent inactivity on your behalf?

Resources for Further Study

Books

Victor Venfield, *Trigeminal Neuralgia: Living with Trigeminal Neuralgia, A Practical Guide* (n.p.: IMB, 2014).
Philip Yancey, *Disappointment with God* (Grand Rapids: Zondervan, 1997).
————, *Where Is God When It Hurts?* (Grand Rapids: Zondervan, 2002).

Articles

Mark McGinniss, "The Courage to Live," *Baptist Bulletin*, March/April 2014.
————, "Going Forward," *Summit*, Spring 2013.
————, "When Surgery Fails," *Kindred Spirit*, Winter 2012.

Websites

Mark McGinniss, *Outside My Door* (blog), https://outsidemydoor.wordpress .com/.
Living with TN, http://www.livingwithtn.org/main.
TN Facial Pain Association, http://fpa-support.org/.
Trigeminal Neuralgia Association UK, *Facing Pain Together*, http://www.tna .org.uk/.

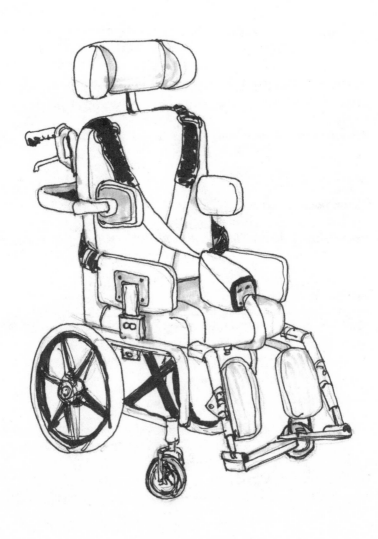

FOUR

Redeeming Disability:
Parenting a Child with Special Needs

MARY KLENTZMAN

> We rejoice in hope of the glory of God. More than that, we
> rejoice in our sufferings, knowing that suffering produces en-
> durance, and endurance produces character, and character pro-
> duces hope, and hope does not put us to shame, because God's
> love has been poured into our hearts through the Holy Spirit
> who has been given to us. (Rom. 5:2b–5, ESV)[1]

When Jonathan was born, the doctor knew right away that there were problems. Even though this was my fifth child, I didn't register that his head was smaller than normal; I had accepted years before that newborns don't always look beautiful. I held Jonathan briefly before they took him away, claiming they were going to bathe and weigh him.

The pregnancy had not been typical—but what pregnancy is? At four months, our small-town doctor told us that our due date was considerably off. He didn't have an ultrasound machine, but he was confident that because of the size of the baby, this child would be arriving at least a couple of months before the original October date. Unfortunately, he would not be able to help us through the remainder of my pregnancy: he was giving up his obstetrical practice.

So on top of preparing for a new baby in the household, we began search-

---

1   All Scripture quotations are from the NKJV unless otherwise indicated. All emphases are mine.

ing for another doctor—and I was pretty particular. I visited new doctors every month, asking a great number of questions to see if they met specs. Because we hadn't settled on a physician until the seventh month, no one did an ultrasound. By that time, the baby's size seemed to fit the original due date and there was always a strong, healthy heartbeat. No need for concern.

On Labor Day (how fitting!) 1988, I had contractions all day, but nothing settled into a pattern, and it was a month before the due date. However, I was alarmed the following morning when I discovered what I thought was a prolapsed cord, which could cut off the baby's oxygen and kill him or her. My husband jumped into action, working to pack up the kids, keep me in a reclining position, get the kids to the neighbors, and rush me to the hospital forty-five minutes away. The whole way I was praying that my baby would still be alive when we got to the hospital.

When we arrived, the medical crew speedily hooked me up to an external fetal monitor and turned up the speaker to listen for signs of life. Right away we heard a strong, healthy, perfectly beating heart. What a relief! When they examined me, though, they discovered that what I had thought was a prolapsed cord was actually the twin brother of the child whose heartbeat I could hear. He appeared to have been dead for about four months. We finally understood why the baby had seemed so large at four months and then settled into a more normal size.

But the hospital staff didn't have a clue what to do with me. It was a miracle that I didn't have a horrific infection from carrying a dead child that long, but I wasn't in labor. Would the other baby be born in the next few hours, or would he or she wait until closer to the actual due date a month from now? They decided to keep me in the hospital overnight to watch for signs of infection.

My husband had to leave me to get the other kids, so I was alone in the hospital. I sat in the bed pondering the day. Of course, I was sad that my baby was dead. Did God allow this because He knew that I didn't have what it takes to raise twins? On the other hand, I couldn't help but think of God's tenderness with my emotions. He had allowed me to hear one baby's healthy heartbeat before I found out about my other baby's death. The child I had looked forward to for eight months was still alive.

A dear friend who is a Johns Hopkins-trained pediatrician came to visit me in the hospital that night. She was certain that our baby would be born that night.

And she was right. It was quite handy to be able to walk down the hall from my hospital room to the labor room!

After what seemed an eternity (I got pretty miffed that they were taking so long to bring me my baby), a kind pediatrician entered our room. God provided us with a precious Christian doctor to share some life-changing news. He said, "I wish I could tell you everything is okay with your baby, but this wouldn't be honest. Your baby has a very small head, which indicates that he likely has considerable brain injury. I am so sorry."

We named him Jonathan, which means "gift from God." We had no idea how prophetic this name would be, though the gift wasn't at all like what I would ever have chosen had I had the chance. It was far more precious and wonderful.

That evening a group of friends came to the hospital to see us. One of them had had a similar experience with one twin that didn't survive. She and the living twin had to fight a terrible infection even though the deceased child had only been dead a day or two before the birth. Her surviving son, I knew, had cerebral palsy as a result.

Later that night, when I was once again alone in my hospital room, I cried out to God, telling Him that I didn't see how I could handle taking care of a child with special needs. I was barely keeping my nose above water with the responsibilities of raising four typical kids; how could I add a child who would need extra time and attention? I began looking through my Bible, seeking verses of encouragement. I wanted a verse to light up on the page that said, "All is well. God will heal your baby soon and the world will see how mighty our God is!"

However, what came to mind were words I had memorized years earlier by putting them to a tune: "My soul, wait only upon God, and silently submit to Him. For my hope and expectation are from Him. He only is my rock and my salvation. He is my strength and my fortress. I shall not be moved" (based on Ps. 62:1–2). God knew well ahead of time that I would need to be reminded of these words again and again throughout my life.

Still, in the days ahead I comforted myself by remembering a documentary I had seen about a group of people who were born with hydrocephalus (excessive fluid on the brain) many years before MRIs were invented. When the technology became available for them—after they had their master's degrees and started their families—the MRIs revealed that great portions of their brains were damaged. The remaining parts of their brains had adapted to take over the function of the injured parts. I rested in the possibility that this could be Jonathan's experience, too.

I was well aware that God was sustaining me during the first weeks after Jonathan was born. At our small-town church, I saw more sadness for me in the eyes of my friends than I was actually experiencing myself. They were responding to God's mandate to bear one another's burdens by bearing *my* burdens in prayer. I will forever be grateful for them.

When Jonathan was two months old, a bright red, nickel-sized spot appeared on his neck. It looked like it might have been a bruise from a car seat strap, but I decided to get it checked in case it needed attention. Since it didn't seem serious, I took Jonathan to a little clinic close to our rural home rather than the larger medical facility forty-five minutes away. The clinic doctor hadn't seen Jonathan before, but since it was a small town, he had heard about what was going on with us. As I sat in the waiting room holding Jonathan and reading a magazine, a thought came to me out of the blue: "Things are not as they appear." Later I would remember and cling to this thought.

The doctor could tell right away that the mark on Jonathan's neck was a harmless hemangioma that likely would disappear within a few years. But his next statements took the wind out of me. He asked, "Did Jonathan's other doctors tell you that his head will never get any bigger than it is right now?" Now, Jonathan's head was *very* small. And my husband and his family are *very* tall and muscular. So what came to mind was Jonathan as a teenager with a tiny head on top of a huge, football-player-sized body. Would my son really look like some freak from *Men in Black*? The doctor went on: "You and your husband need to consider placing this baby in an institution. You've got all your other kids to think about." He looked down at Jonathan and continued, "You've got to understand—a kid without a brain can't do anything." I thought I might pass out, but I didn't want to cry in front of this man. Before I could gather my things to leave, the doctor brought an older doctor into the exam room. As if to comfort me, this second doctor said, "For thirty years I've been treating a set of Siamese twins who couldn't be separated."

"What are they doing today?" I asked, hoping to hear encouraging accounts of their careers as CPAs, novelists, or in some other respectable profession. Instead, the doctor lowered his head and muttered, "They work in the circus." Men in Black freak, here we go. "Things are not as they appear . . ."

When Jonathan was six months old, a physical therapist working with him mentioned something about cerebral palsy. I asked, "Does he have cerebral palsy?" She looked shocked that I didn't know. I suppose the other professionals had all assumed that someone else had broken the diagnosis to us.

My older children couldn't have been happier to have a new baby in the house. Though the typical newborn characteristics that most babies grow out of ever so quickly continued with no end in sight, Jonathan's siblings took it all without question. A stranger asked six-year-old Jill what was "wrong" with her little brother. She replied, "Oh nothing, he just has cereal palsy." She genuinely did not see a defect.

The brain injury caused Jonathan to have severe, unrelenting muscle cramps that made him very uncomfortable and fussy while lying down. But he couldn't sit up by himself, either—his little body would stiffen uncontrollably, causing his back to arch with spasms. We tried placing him in specialized equipment, like a wheelchair or corner chair, that would strap him in an upright sitting position, but hard surfaces stimulated horribly painful spasms. When he was five years old, we discovered medicine that provided some relief from the spasms. But until that time, Jonathan was held almost twenty-four hours a day. During the day, his siblings, who were homeschooled, and I took turns holding him. We would excuse the child who was holding Jonathan from doing chores, so the kids fought over who got to hold him. I'm confident that this idea was from the Lord, because it kept the siblings from resenting their brother's constant need for care. Even so, there were times when the older children complained that they had more responsibilities than their friends. Though other members of my family expressed deep concern that the siblings were going to be forever terribly scarred by their experiences, I had to cling to God's promise that He would work all of this for His good in their lives.

Nothing better illustrates God's faithfulness in this promise than the way Jonathan "taught" Kimberly, our oldest, to play the piano. For years I had longed for my children to learn to play the piano, because this skill had been such a blessing in my life. I had served for many years as church pianist and later accompanied my family as we sang in churches, in camps, and in events. But more than this, sitting at the piano to play and sing praises to Jesus was therapeutic and strengthened my relationship with Him. I desired the same experience for my children, but it seemed that there was no way for this to happen. Though I had given others piano lessons for years, I couldn't find the time to teach my own children. Between taking Jonathan to physical, occupational, and speech therapies and doctor appointments, along with homeschooling the oldest three children, preparing food, doing laundry, and cleaning, I couldn't squeeze another activity into our schedule. And did I ever feel guilty about it! Nor could we afford to pay for the kids to take piano lessons from someone else. After much frustration and self-condemnation, I did what I should have done in the first place: I relinquished my desire to my heavenly Father and told Him, "If my children need the skill of playing the piano in their futures, I trust You to provide the training they need."

Remember when Paul told the Ephesians that God is able to do exceedingly more abundantly than anything we ask or think (Eph. 3:20)? This was one of those occasions. There was no way I could have thought to ask God to do what He did.

Around Jonathan's second birthday, we discovered the reason for his long hours of crying in pain: he was cutting six teeth at the same time. Because the cerebral palsy made his arms and hands uncontrollably stiff and straight like little tree limbs, he was unable to put teething toys or food in his mouth as most toddlers do. The brain injury also took away his ability to chew foods. These challenges dramatically lengthened the time it took for teeth to break through the gums.

As a result, my normally cheerful child was especially miserable most of the time—except when I held him in my lap and played the piano. Experience had shown me that even when he had excruciating ear infections, when I took him to the piano, his stiff little body would relax in my arms as I played, and his anguished face would turn to a smile as he began cooing a song of satisfaction and peace. But cutting teeth was a long process, and as much as I wanted to, I just didn't have time to spend hours each day at the piano. Our daughter Kimberly, who was twelve years old at this time, had taken a few months of piano lessons in the first grade. I asked her to take a turn at the piano soothing Jonathan. At my request she propped him in her lap, held him in place with her elbows so that he didn't fall from side to side, then began to play songs from her third-grade piano lesson book. She played for hours that day—and every day for the following weeks and months. During this time I would occasionally offer her new songs to play, from classical to jazz to hymn arrangements, with increasingly higher levels of difficulty. Six months later, it dawned on us that a miracle had occurred. Kimberly had progressed from that third-grade piano book to playing music I had played in college—all with a little person in her lap whom the world considered to have little to no value. During the coming years, Jonathan taught his sister Jill to play the piano, too! Both girls later had opportunities to take real piano lessons and went on to win major national piano competitions. Even more importantly, God taught them through this experience that people are valuable, no matter what their abilities. During four years of graduate school, Jill played the piano three and four days each week at a nursing home because she knew the wonderful impact music has on people who are hurting.

One of the hardest characteristics of disability is that it never goes away. An illness like flu or cancer draws family and friends to bring meals and provides a place on the church prayer list. But long-term trials and afflictions get old for everyone involved, and it becomes embarrassing to bring up the same need for the thousandth time, though the trial assuredly still exists. Recalling blessings like Kimberly's and Jill's piano playing has provided encouragement and faith to help us get through considerable challenges that have no end in sight.

Grieving and Disability

When Jonathan was three years old, I attended training about the grieving process that is typical for parents who have children with disabilities. I felt such comfort when I gained a rational label for the feelings I had. Prior to this, I would scold myself for having emotions that seemed silly—even contrary to how a Christian should feel. I hadn't realized that it was normal for parents whose children have special needs to go through stages of grief similar to those one encounters with a terminal illness and after the death of a loved one. Parents like me grieve the loss of the child they thought they were going to have—the one who grows up to play soccer or be a dancer or pianist. They also grieve the loss of the life they had dreamed of having—the life where their children grow up, become independent, and where they have free time to participate in activities of their choosing.

This grieving includes shock with the initial diagnosis, denial, anger, bargaining, depression, and acceptance. It differs from the grief surrounding a death in that with death, there is finality. With disability, the stages of grief can be experienced again and again with each new diagnosis or missed developmental milestone. Sometimes the emotions come totally out of the blue—I experienced them when two-year-old Jonathan got his first wheelchair and when his hospital bed was delivered. On these and numerous other occasions, the reality that something was terribly wrong hit me like a punch to the stomach, and the subsequent sadness caught me completely off guard.

Lack of sleep exacerbates grieving. It's no wonder that sleep deprivation is used as a means of torture for prisoners of war because it brutalizes one's whole person. Jonathan's sleeping habits, as with many children with special needs, are much like those of a very high-maintenance newborn—a newborn who never grows up. For most of his life we've needed to get up with him many times each night and sometimes for hours at a time.

God has been ever so faithful even through this. He has given supernatural strength when there shouldn't have been an ounce of energy to take the next step. And there have been occasions when He showed up to provide divine encouragement when it was needed most.

God's Great Love

One of these times was during those first five years of Jonathan's life when he needed to be held constantly. The children and I took turns during the day. And because my husband had to get up early each morning to go to work, I took the night shift. It took hours for Jonathan to fall asleep. I would sit up with him facing me, cross-legged in my lap, so that my body would serve as a barrier to keep his legs bent to break up the spasticity and help him relax. I would jostle him with my knees until he gave up and went to sleep. Then I would carefully lie down with his head still in the crook of my arm. Eight to ten times during the night, when he would stiffen with muscle spasm pain, I would bend his knees again and jostle him with my arms to help him go back to sleep.

One evening, when exhaustion and discouragement gripped me in such a way that I thought I couldn't keep going, I cried out to God asking for His intervention. I had often prayed for Him to heal Jonathan. I reasoned that such a miraculous healing would bring great glory to His name. When people saw a child who had never been able to walk or talk get up and run around and tell them about Jesus, they would *have* to believe in this wonder-working God. And further, if Jonathan were healed, I would be freed up to do so much more for Him—like teach Bible studies or mentor and help other young mothers.

But I didn't pray for healing that evening. That evening, I just needed encouragement. I just needed to feel His presence—to feel His arms around me holding me—while I held a child who was struggling to go to sleep. I'll never forget the way He answered my cry. He revealed to me that, just like we held Jonathan twenty-four hours a day, He holds us every moment of every day whether we feel it or not. God reminded me we were not motivated to hold Jonathan by his beauty, his intelligence, his ability, or what he would do for us in return. We were compelled to hold and comfort him simply because we adored this little person. In the same way, God's motivation for drawing close to embrace us is not based on the way we look, how smart we are, or what we do or possibly could do for Him. His sole motivation is His deep compassion for us. This glimpse of God's love for me has carried me through many long, sleepless nights and challenging days.

More Children, More Lessons

My husband and I were blessed with two more children, Andrew and Michael, who were born when Jonathan was five and seven years old. When Andrew was two weeks old, we began traveling fifty miles away twice each week to take Jonathan to a physical therapist who was gifted to work with children with severe disabilities. It was this therapist who noticed some physical problems that Andrew was having. She recommended that we get an MRI of Andrew's brain. As a result, at nineteen months, he was diagnosed with hemiplegic cerebral palsy due to a stroke he had before he was born. It made him weak on his left side; his left hand became his helper hand, and he had an unsteady gait. A speech delay was discovered later. Nonetheless, Andrew's development far surpassed Jonathan's. Andrew was able to sit up by himself, grasp toys, and walk, though he fell frequently. So I was surprised at how difficult it was for me to handle this diagnosis. Before, I tended to downplay other people's challenges, thinking, "Well, at least they can talk, or walk," or whatever the case may be. Now I realized how wrong I had been. No matter the disability, it is like a knife to the heart of parents as they grieve and have great concern about how the disability will impact their child's future. This experience was also a blessed reminder that we mustn't be prideful, thinking "I suffer more than you."

The Body of Christ and Disability

During countless nights rubbing Jonathan's head, repositioning him, or cradling him in my arms to relieve pain and help him sleep, I've pondered the pro-life stance of the conservative Christian church, a conviction that I strongly hold. My view as a mom of a child with special needs has provided me with another conviction just as profound: If we are going to urge an expectant mom not to abort her baby, even when she suspects her child has some sort of anomaly, we as Christ-followers had better be there to assist her and her family after the baby is born. And I'm not referring just to a short period after the birth. We must help them through the long haul.

Some parents say that many Christians seem to be "pro-birth" but not "pro-life." Quite honestly, I wonder what I would be like if I hadn't had a child with disabilities. I'm afraid I would have consoled myself that life with a child with special needs must not be that difficult, or that the government or some other group would provide all the help these families need. There are many—including educated professionals—who comfort themselves with thoughts like these. But they are far from the truth. Even if there were unlimited government dollars available and designated to provide assistance for families affected by disabilities, they would not provide a fraction of the support that these families really need. If managed correctly, they might be able to provide funds for wheelchairs, doctor and therapy costs, medications, diapers for older children and adults, feeding tubes, and many of the other large expenses connected with this population. But what about resources to address the isolation, the significant marriage strain and sibling concerns, and the spiritual needs of these families? No government funding can come close to impacting these intense, long-term challenges.

Sadly, many families affected by disabilities can't even find a church that they can attend, much less connect with to grow stronger spiritually, personally, and in their family relationships. Unless these families know ahead of time that there is a special-needs ministry in place, they can't just show up at a church on a Sunday morning and expect that their child with behavioral or medical challenges can be assimilated into a typical Sunday school classroom or sit through a church service. Sadly, the majority of parents who have visited a church expecting that at least in God's house they would be welcomed have come away devastated by rejection. Numerous parents have told me that they have been kicked out of churches—one family had been kicked out of five—because of their children's disabilities.

Church leaders typically never consider the possibility that families affected by disability live in the vicinity of their church. After all, they don't see these families at church on Sundays. Churches have no idea that there is an enormous mission field of families who have a family member with special needs. And these houses of worship are unaware that their facilities, programs, and culture are fraught with barriers too high for most families impacted by disability.

God has used my experience as Jonathan's mom—and the opportunities this role has afforded me to interact with other parents who have children with disabilities—to develop a deep desire to help other families like mine. For the first decade of Jonathan's life, I could barely keep my own nose above water, much less try to help someone else. But the fervency of this longing only grew, though there was little prospect that I would ever be able to come up for air long enough to accomplish anything that would make a difference for good in someone else's life. For years I was so busy taking care of children, household needs, and a variety of medical appointments for Jonathan, that I was unable to help anyone else. And this, quite honestly, was discouraging.

But God, in His faithfulness and mercy, was obviously well aware of my hurts and desires, and He ministered to me exactly where I needed it most.

The Blessings of Hope

When Jonathan was about ten years old, the word "hope" repeatedly came to my mind as I was talking with God. At first I thought God was nudging me to pray for someone named Hope. But as I prayed, it became clear to me that God was speaking to my heart about hope—that I had inadvertently lost all hope. So with His nudging, I began searching for Scriptures that refer to hope. To my amazement, I discovered a great number. Here are a few (followed by my comments):

- We rejoice in the *hope* of the glory of God. Not only so, but we also rejoice in our sufferings, because we know that suffering produces perseverance, perseverance, character, and character, *hope*. And *hope* does not disappoint us, because God has poured out his love into our hearts by the Holy Spirit, whom he has given us (Rom. 5:2–5, NIV 1984). Who would have thought that suffering would end up producing hope in our lives!
- Against all *hope*, Abraham *in hope* believed and so became the father of many nations (Rom. 4:18, NIV). He had hope that was "against all hope" to believe that God could intervene and accomplish in his life by providing a child for him and Sarah in their old age.
- Those who *hope* in [the Lord] will not be disappointed (Isa. 49:23, NIV). How encouraging to know that the Lord will never let us down.
- Faith, *hope*, and love, but the greatest of these is love (1 Cor. 13:13). I had never discovered that hope is one of the top three things listed in 1 Corinthians 13.
- Now faith is the substance of things *hoped* for, the evidence of things not seen (Heb. 11:1). This verse reveals that hope is the basis for faith.

While it seems that many professionals are afraid of offering "false hope," God desires that we hope in Him. In a most grace-filled, compassionate way, God showed me that not only is it not foolish to hope for His intervention, but hope is important for our faith. And for most parents who have children with special needs, there is no hope except in Jesus.

Getting a glimpse of the important part hope plays in our faith had a significant impact on strengthening my relationship with Jesus. I began to look forward with hope and expectation as to what God was going to do next in my life and in the lives of each member of my family. And as the Scripture says, I was not disappointed.

New Ministry

God began opening doors for me to help others in ways that I couldn't have imagined earlier. I was approached about directing a nonprofit that provides services to families who have children with disabilities. Miraculously, Jonathan, at eleven years old, had grown healthy enough to go to school for the first time, which freed me to work away from home. Through this position God gave me a way to provide considerable, practical help for other families like mine.

As the organization's first full-time employee, I had opportunities to initiate new resources and grow the existing ones that positively impact families. My experience as a parent of a child with disabilities meant that I understood their needs and cost-effective measures that could be put into place to meet those needs. We provided a variety of resources such as respite (providing fun activities for children with disabilities and their siblings while their parents get a much-needed break), medical supplies and equipment, and training for parents on topics of interest (special education, behavior management, available state resources, etc.). We provided a childcare during the trainings, because I knew that many parents couldn't attend without it. We also trained pediatric residents and other medical personnel to work more sensitively and effectively with children with special needs and their families. Another outreach program was created to educate local churches about the need to welcome families affected by disability and gave the churches tips on how to develop special-needs ministries.

During this time, I inadvertently fell into advocacy roles. God continues to use my experience as a parent of a child with disabilities to bring awareness to state legislators and leaders in Health and Human Services and Agencies regarding policies that adversely impact people of all ages who have disabilities. And on numerous occasions, God has been faithful to use my testimony to move on the hearts and minds of state leaders to change policies and create new laws to make life a bit easier for those who live with disability every day—and often save the state money at the same time. I've been able to serve on statewide advisory councils that have made significant positive changes impacting a multitude of people with disabilities and their families from all over the state.

After ten years directing the nonprofit in central Texas, God provided me with other opportunities to fulfill the desire of my heart to minister to families affected by disability. These included directing the large disability ministry at Prestonwood Baptist Church, directing the Texas Joni and Friends office, and now directing a distinctly Christian home and day program for adults with disabilities. I am confident that God used Jonathan to develop this passion I have for helping other families affected by disability. And He alone has made it possible for me to accomplish things that I would have never been able to do had I not had Jonathan in my life.

Continually Needing to Learn and Grow in Faith

Our Lord continues to intervene on our behalf, helping us to grow in our faith and relationships with Him. It is common that the greatest lessons are given and grasped through the most difficult times. When people with disabilities reach the age of 21, though their conditions haven't changed, the available resources alter dramatically. Individuals with special needs are entitled by the government to public school until the year of their twenty-first birthday. If those individuals qualify for nursing care through Medicaid, they receive this benefit until the day they turn 21.

For a typical young man turning 21, the occasion is a happy one, bringing him close to graduation and settling into a career. As we were planning for Jonathan's transition, however, grief raised its ugly head again. On top of this, Jonathan got very sick with upper respiratory problems that degenerated into bilateral pneumonia and a week-long hospital stay. The antibiotics caused serious problems with his digestion with subsequent nutritional deficiencies. All of this led to a dangerous pressure sore. At the same time, another son was struggling with severe depression.

I prayed. No, I begged. I felt that if I could just pray harder, pray longer, maybe learn to pray better, that God would move on our behalf. And I blamed myself. I thought that if I had prayed harder and better, these bad things wouldn't have happened.

Then one day God, in a very tender, non-condemning way, showed me that I had made fixing my circumstances an idol in my life. I was treating God as a means to make my problems go away instead of as my first love, my all-in-all. He also showed me that by blaming myself for the struggles that

Jonathan and my other family members were experiencing, I was taking responsibilities that weren't mine to take.

With deep sadness for my sin, I repented of this idolatry. The transformative power of my loving, forgiving Lord reached in and changed my heart and my thinking. I fell in love with Him again. I discovered that I can totally trust and rest in His sovereignty, because out of His great, unfathomable love for us, He is able to work everything—even the most difficult of circumstances—for good for those of us who love Him and are called according to His purpose. In His graciousness, God showed me that He is with me, giving me strength to get through. And I discovered that a precious love relationship with Him is not a consolation prize for situations that we consider to be bad.

More Lessons Learned

When my youngest son was ten years old, he and I had a rare opportunity to take a road trip, just the two of us. Along the way we discussed many topics, including the way all things really do work together for good to those who love God and are called according to His purpose. We talked about the extraordinary blessings that have come to us because Jonathan is a part of our family. We've met people we would never have met. We've experienced things we would never have experienced. Then I said, "You know, Michael, sometimes God allows challenges in our lives that are bigger than we can handle to force us to trust Him." Immediately Michael responded, "No, Mom, that's not right."

"Excuse me?" I replied, somewhat incensed. He said, "God doesn't force us to do anything. We have to choose whether we will trust Him or not." I was stunned for a moment; I had to agree that my young son was absolutely correct. There is little doubt, however, that a seemingly unending barrage of responsibilities can, indeed, cause us to recognize that there is no way we can accomplish them in our own strength and abilities. Our need for God becomes ever more evident. And by trusting Him through these, we discover what He says in His word: that nothing is impossible with Him (Luke 1:37) and that His strength is made perfect in weakness (2 Cor. 12:9). But yes, we do get to choose whether we will trust Him or not.

I have seen wonderful examples of God's faithfulness in the blessings Jonathan's siblings have received from their experience growing up with a brother who has special needs. I strongly believe that because of Jonathan they easily accept and feel compassion for others who have physical, intellectual, and behavioral differences. All have volunteered for numerous organizations that serve people with special needs. One son even met his future wife at a camp for children with special needs.

Jonathan is a greatly treasured member of our family. All three of our married children included Jonathan as a groomsman in their weddings; he was best man in both of our sons' weddings. Also, all of Jonathan's brothers and sisters have had assignments in school to tell about someone who has had a significant positive impact in their lives. All have chosen Jonathan.

Romans 8:28 tells us that "all things work together for good to those who love God and are called according to His purpose." There come times in all of our lives when we are tempted to doubt this fact. We can't imagine that any good can come from intense, long-term difficulties. Through the years, God has revealed many blessings and insights that He has made available to our family directly out of experience with trials and afflictions. Our suffering has given us:

1. *The ability to comfort others.* Any time a Christian experiences the death of a loved one, a rebellious child, unemployment, or disability, this person becomes commissioned to a new ministry. Their credibility to others becomes heightened, and their witness bears a weightier impact. Parents who have children with disabilities find it far easier to receive comfort and assurance of God's faithfulness and love from others who have walked through similar challenges.

2. *A greater knowledge of God.* Just like Abraham got to know God as Jehovah Jireh, his provider, when God provided the ram in the bushes during Abraham's great need, we get to know God and His attributes far more intimately during times of great need. Two months after Jonathan was born, my husband's job ended, leaving him without full-time employment for the following 18 months. During this time we received a notice that our hospital bill had been paid by an anonymous donor. Our freezer stayed full and our refrigerator was never empty. We discovered who our Provider actually is in ways that we could not have grasped without this experience.

3. *A clearer focus on the Lord.* The Lord uses times of trouble to teach timeless lessons. I always feel like life's significant struggles provide an effective remedy for spiritual attention deficit disorder. God has my undivided attention when I am desperate for His intervention in my

life. I diligently seek answers from His Word and spend more time in fervent prayer.

4. *Faith-building memories.* It becomes easier to trust God when we have previously witnessed His wonderful acts of mercy in our lives. As we face a new trial, what a gift it is to be able to look back and remember the ways God has intervened on our behalf in the past!

I admire people who journal consistently. The closest thing I have done to journaling is to write my prayers—sometimes at the end of my rope, sometimes in rejoicing and thanksgiving for the amazing things God has done. I have done this once, twice, maybe ten times each year for the past twenty years. At times I added Scriptures and insights I thought God was giving me at the time. All of these prayers and thoughts are in a well-worn three-ring binder. I recently read through the whole notebook for the first time. What a faith-builder to see the multitude of answered prayers, the faithfulness of God, the hope that God can accomplish what appears impossible—in ways we would never have been able to imagine! It was evident that through every challenging experience, God, in His mercy, grace, and power, got us through—and He did it victoriously.

We won't know until we get to heaven all of the gifts God has bestowed through Jonathan, but He has certainly astounded us with those that we've been able to see and recognize here on earth. Who could have imagined when our little "gift from God" was born that he would impact our lives in such extraordinary ways? Even with our finite minds, we can observe that Jonathan's life has great purpose—exactly as he was created. He has been the best kind of gift to all of us.

Discussion Questions

1. What questions could a family member affected by disability be asked in order to sensitively gain information regarding how to effectively help them with not only their physical needs, but also their spiritual and emotional needs?

2. What is one change that could be made to make your church more welcoming to families affected by disabilities?

3. Have there been times in your life that there appeared to be no hope for you to get through a difficult situation, yet God intervened in an unexpected way to get you through it victoriously? Share one of your experiences.

Resources for Further Study

Books

Elizabeth J. Bruce and Cynthia L. Schultz, *Nonfinite Loss and Grief* (Baltimore: Paul H. Brookes, 2001).

Erik W. Carter, *Including People with Disabilities in Faith Communities* (Baltimore: Paul H. Brookes, 2007).

Shelly Chapin, *Counselors, Comforters, and Friends: Establishing a Caregiving Ministry in Your Church* (Wheaton, IL: Scripture Press, 1992).

Emily Colson, *Dancing with Max* (Grand Rapids: Zondervan, 2010).

Melanie Fowler, *Look at My Eyes* (Dallas: Brown Christian Press, 2011).

Cheri Fuller and Louise Tucker Jones, *Extraordinary Kids: Nurturing and Championing Your Child with Special Needs* (Colorado Springs, CO: Focus on the Family, 1997).

Stephanie Hubach, *Same Lake, Different Boat: Coming Alongside People Touched by Disability* (Phillipsburg, NJ: P & R, 2006).

Timothy Keller, *Generous Justice: How God's Grace Makes Us Just* (New York: Riverhead, 2010).

Stanley D. Klein and Kim Schive, *You Will Dream New Dreams* (New York: Kensington, 2011).

Jim Pierson, *Exceptional Teaching: A Comprehensive Guide for Including Students with Disabilities* (Cincinnati: Standard, 2002).

Lisa Simmons, *I Would Have Said Yes: A Family's Journey with Autism* (Bloomington, IN: WestBow, 2012).

Joni Eareckson Tada, *A Place of Healing* (Colorado Springs, CO: David C. Cook, 2010).

Websites

Timothy Keller, "A Christian's Happiness" http://sermons2.redeemer.com/sermons/christians-happiness.

———, Born into Hope"http://sermons2.redeemer.com/sermons/born-hope.

———, "Thy Will Be Done" http://sermons2.redeemer.com/sermons/thy-will-be-done.

FIVE

Redeeming Trauma:
The Trials and Triumphs of Emergency Responders

STEVE CALVERT

We went through fire and flood, but you brought us to a place
of great abundance. (Ps. 66:12) [1]

I became acquainted with trauma at the age of 14. My dad and I were
loading the lawnmower in the car to mow a widow lady's yard when we
heard the screams. As we ran down the street, we saw our neighbor on
her front porch, screaming in terror. All we could make out was, "Upstairs!
In the bedroom!" We sprinted up the stairs to find her husband lying across
the bed, lifeless. He had put a gun in his mouth and pulled the trigger. Dad
sent me back home to get help. I tried to call for an ambulance, but I was
shaking so much from the horrific scene that I couldn't get my finger into
the hole on the dial of our rotary telephone. My mom took over that job and
I ran back to the scene.

Little did I know that God would use me to work with hundreds of other
families experiencing the worst day of their lives. It still amazes me that He
took a young country preacher right out of Bible college and led me into
ministry, both as a pastor and as a fire department chaplain, firefighter, and
emergency medical technician (EMT). This has been my calling for the past
thirty-five years.

---

1   All Scripture quotations are taken from the NKJV unless otherwise indicated.

Baptism by Fire

My first emergency call was to a secluded country home in north Alabama in the middle of the night. Our small community, Somerville, had a post office, a caution light, and a gas station. By the time a house fire got big enough for a neighbor to see it and call it in, it would be raging. Such was the case on this call.

As we approached the burning house, my heart sank. I knew this old, white-framed house; I'd been in it many times. It belonged to one of the families in our church—a dad, a mom, and two teenage boys. All of the cars were in the yard. "They must be home," I thought. The back of the house was engulfed in flames.

I jumped out of the truck, put the air pack on, and ran to the front door while other firefighters were pulling hose. After banging on the door and getting no response, I felt the door, checked for signs of backdraft, and kicked the door open. I found myself face-to-face with the younger teenage son. He stood just inside the door with a double-barrel shotgun pointing straight at my mask. He was delirious and scared; I believe God's intervention kept him from pulling the trigger. We were able to awaken the other three family members and get them out of the house before flames consumed it.

Life Heats Up

The years have given me countless opportunities to walk with families through tragedies. I have pastored churches in Alabama, Georgia, and Texas, but one thing has been consistent: as soon as my wife, Gina, and I moved to work with a new church, I would contact the local fire department. If it was a volunteer department, or if they used trained volunteers, I would join the department and get to work.

The work allowed me as the new minister in town to get to know great people committed to serving others (firefighters/EMTs and their families) and also exposed me to those in my community who were experiencing tragedy. Whether I was serving as minister, firefighter/EMT, or fire chaplain, my goal was always to glorify God and be His hands, His feet, His hugs, His tears, and occasionally His words to those who were suffering. Whether I was working on the side of the highway to extricate someone trapped in a vehicle, caring for a teenager who had attempted suicide (or their family, if they succeeded), or sitting in a hospital as a family said goodbye, I came to see that God was always there.

Much of my life has been spent with precious souls whose lives—and often faith—are shattered. Yet I have also seen incredible resilience as individuals and families overcome and deal with such tragedies. That dichotomy began to shape my understanding of how God works through pain and suffering in our lives.

In August 2001, we moved to Coppell, Texas, to work with a church that was an oasis of healing to many who had been traumatized by life—and by religion. We saw God work in amazing ways as people encountered Jesus in a real way for the first time. Many who came to know the Lord had completely given up on God. I also became the chaplain for the Coppell Fire Department, a role I have been privileged to fill for years since.

In July 2007, I was asked to be the campus pastor of a growing multisite church in the north Dallas area. As we tried to impact the community for Christ, the campus grew to just under one thousand attending our three weekend services. I felt blessed ministering to the believers who were doing life together, raising up and training small group leaders, and working alongside the first responders in my home community.

In 2008, Gina and I experienced a shattering financial tragedy of our own. A close family friend, a Christian to whom we had entrusted all of our finances for the previous fifteen years, was convicted of running a Ponzi scheme. All of our life savings, 401(k), and kids' college funds were gone. In addition, since we'd been drawing from our investments for the previous five years to supplement our income when I changed churches, the receiver with the courts ordered us to pay back $45,000.

We've carried back-breaking debt ever since. We moved to a house half the size of our previous home and then to another house half the size of that when the last of our three children left for college. Since day one of our marriage, we'd always tithed 10 percent and had tried to be faithful stewards with our finances. I could not understand why God would allow such a thing to happen when we were devoted to serving Him and trying to follow His principles.

Tragedy Brings a New Direction

In April 2013, our world and ministry focus changed dramatically. I was asked by the Texas Corps of Fire Chaplains and the Federation of Fire Chaplains to help with the relief efforts at the fertilizer plant explosion in West, Texas, where we'd lost twelve firefighter/emergency medical services (EMS) first responders. Hundreds of homes were destroyed, along with a forty-unit apartment complex and a middle school.

We had twelve funerals to prepare. Fire department honor guards were posted with each family and each body until the burials. In addition to working with the grieving families, we were challenged with managing the overwhelming media coverage and the protestors who believed that these deaths were God's outpouring of wrath because of the moral state of our country.

West was a close-knit small town; everyone who died was either family or close friends to those in the community. In addition to the families whose loved ones had paid the ultimate sacrifice to save others' lives, there were those whose homes had been destroyed. I spent time with these families during the day. At night, I would drop by the fire station, where the surviving first responders would come out of the shadows to congregate away from the media. It broke my heart to see them deal with grief as well as guilt.

Late one night, I met a courageous young couple who had saved many lives. He was a first responder and she was a trauma nurse. They had seen the smoke at the plant and had frantically evacuated the homes and apartment complex in their neighborhood before the explosion. He was going to help with the firefighting efforts when the explosion occurred, rocking his truck. I spent many hours with them. He wrote me later and told me that before he met me that night, he had decided to take his life. He'd lost close friends in the blast, including one who was like a brother. The couple ultimately divorced.

I was particularly touched by the older gentleman who owned the fertilizer plant. He was a farmer and a devout Christian. He had bought the plant several years earlier when the owners had planned to close it down. He did not want the workers to lose their jobs, and he had been concerned about the farmers for hundreds of miles around who, like himself, depended on it for their crops. The man had never taken a dime of payment from the plant, his son-in-law informed me.

The man and his wife grieved. For weeks, they spent every day at their local church serving food to victims and collecting clothes and other items for the hundreds of families—their neighbors—who had lost their homes. The owner and his wife did not feel that they could go out into the community or to any of the funerals, as they would be a distraction to recovery efforts and the other families who were grieving. With tears in his eyes, the owner told me that every one of the men who had died was like a son to him; he'd watched them grow up and have families.

After spending two weeks on the ground in West, I made many trips back when the Bureau of Alcohol, Tobacco, Firearms, and Explosives (ATF) and other federal and state organizations had critical and sensitive information to share with each of the families. I became close with many of the families; we stay in contact to this day.

Crisis in the Fire Service

It was after the explosion in West that I began to learn some startling statistics regarding the fire service. The suicide rate for firefighters was 30 percent higher than that of the general population, and the divorce rate was 85 percent. The year 2014 saw more firefighters lost to suicide than to line of duty deaths. The region of west Texas had at least seven suicides by firefighters in the first half of 2015 alone. The numbers are startling and seem to be growing. Some of the larger departments are dealing with it in epic proportions.

The Lord used these events to lead me away from full-time pastoring. Gina and I took a prayerful leap of faith and started Champion Responders, a ministry devoted to helping those in the fire/EMS service.

Following the fertilizer plant explosion, the fire chief in Coppell asked me to put together a training program for our department on mental resilience and dealing with post-traumatic stress. I devoted two and a half months to creating the initial training, drawing heavily from the International Critical Incident Stress Foundation and the Marine Corps training manual for combat veterans preparing for or just returning from deployment. The training is called *In for the Long Haul* and is devoted to helping first responders prepare mentally, spiritually, and emotionally for a lifelong career of exposure to trauma. We rolled it out to the department, and the Lord began to open doors for the message to spread.

Around the same time, I received a call from Fire Chief Bobby Halton, the editor-in-chief of two of the most influential periodicals in the fire service, *Fire Engineering* and *Fire Rescue*. He also runs the largest annual fire service conference, the Fire Department Instructors Conference (FDIC). Chief Halton asked me to bring the four-hour training to the upcoming FDIC conference where there would be more than 30,000 attendees from all over the world. "This message is one that our industry needs to hear," he said.

To be able to bring the spiritual message of what we do to firefighters throughout the nation and even to other countries was *huge*. Chief Halton has also asked me to write for both of his magazines from the viewpoint of a trauma chaplain. I have presented the training at the past two FDIC conferences, and now more fire departments and fire training organizations are asking for the training. I could never have imagined having this platform to address the spiritual component of what we do as emergency responders.

The Need for Trained Chaplains

After West, I was asked to serve on the board of directors for the Texas Corps of Fire Chaplains, the Texas chapter of the International Federation of Fire Chaplains. I was charged with raising up and mentoring new fire department chaplains throughout the state of Texas. I also became an instructor for the Federation of Fire Chaplains, training and certifying new chaplains in how to effectively minister to those in crisis, especially to firefighters and emergency responders.

Ministering to family members in the wake of trauma is one of the most challenging things we do, yet it offers an opportunity to minister God's grace, love, comfort, and support to those who are hurting. Unfortunately, many well-meaning people serving in this role (including me in the early days) can do more harm than good by the things they say to those who are hurting.

During the West tragedy, I had seen firsthand the problem of untrained chaplains who show up when disaster strikes and end up doing more harm than good, at least with some. One of the surviving responders at West told his fire chief, "If another one of these people comes up and tries to put their arms around me and tell me God loves me, I'm going to punch them in the face." As well-meaning as they may be, these untrained chaplains often use the tragedy to promote their particular brand of faith—to convert people in the midst of a catastrophe. Some of these groups have actually been asked to leave disaster scenes, including the 9/11 and West disasters. I have learned that ambassadors of Christ have to be very careful in how we comfort people; we must not come across as self-serving. The key in those moments is to be with those who are in pain and to offer a ministry of presence, comfort, and hope. If this ministry is done effectively, God will open the door when the time is right to explore matters of faith and related questions.

There is a time and place for everything (Eccl. 3:4). Job's friends did a wonderful job of ministering to him when they tore their clothes, covered their heads with ashes, and sat silently, mourning with him for seven days and nights. Where they blew it was when they opened their mouths and started trying to explain God to a grief-stricken man in the middle of his trauma.

As a critical incident stress management facilitator, I have worked with fire departments throughout the Dallas-Fort Worth metroplex when they have run especially traumatic calls. These have included multiple deaths at a house fire involving children, suicides, drownings, auto accidents resulting in child fatalities, and extreme violence—including the case of two women who did unspeakable things to their children and themselves because "God told me to." Having visited with the first responders who ran those calls and hearing the gory details, I am amazed that they can continue to live a normal life, much less continue in the work that they do. To persevere as a first responder is a special calling with special gifting from God.

I still vividly remember working with the traumatized caretakers in a nursing home facility where an elderly gentleman who did not want to live anymore shot himself, and I remember those at hospice care facilities who deal with the trauma of grossly deteriorating bodies that are still alive.

I will never forget the Halloween night a teenage boy in a pickup truck played chicken with a passenger train to impress his girlfriend. The teenager won the first time, then (according to the motorist who saw the whole thing) felt that he could turn around and beat it again. The truck exploded on impact, and fire consumed the pickup. As Gina and I crossed the railroad tracks on the country road, we saw the tracks on fire. I looked to my right and saw between two steep embankments the dark silhouette of a train with a glowing, flaming fire beyond it. By the time I got to the front of the train where the truck was, the whole truck was engulfed in flames. There was no hope for the two young teenagers inside. I will never forget the sight and smell of those two kids in the burning truck. Three days later, sitting in a men's Bible study, one of my friends asked for prayers for a close friend of his who had lost his daughter in a train accident three days before. It was the same event, but it was no accident. I didn't tell him. I couldn't. The senselessness of tragedies like this one weighs heavily on me.

All these events leave a wake of trauma and pain for the victims' families, emergency responders, and even hospital staff. Seeing the cumulative effects of trauma is heartbreaking and reinforces my desire—and that of the Federation of Fire Chaplains—to raise up and train fire/EMS chaplains wherever we can throughout our nation.

Steve Calvert

Suffering for Free: The Plight of the Volunteer

People do not realize how traumatic calls like these are to emergency responders. If you're with a paid fire department, you can go back to the fire house and talk through what just happened. If you're a volunteer firefighter/EMT, you put the trucks back into service as fast as you can. Then you go home, crawl back in bed with your wife, and try to block the sights, smells, and sounds out of your mind so you can get a couple of hours of sleep before getting up to go to work the next day.

Most people don't know that the majority of firefighters in this country are volunteers—men and women willing to lay down their lives to save others, with no pay. They sacrifice their own time and often income for training and firefighter/EMT certifications. The first (all-volunteer) department I worked with did not have the financial ability to provide protective gear for firefighters who worked vehicle accidents on a major country highway, structure and house fires, or wild land fires. My second department issued us protective gear if we were willing to cover half of the cost. All of the firefighters who died in the fertilizer plant explosion in West, Texas, were volunteers. Even a professional firefighter from Dallas, Kenny Harris, was visiting in West and responded to the call as a volunteer.

Triggers

What makes a particular call so traumatic to one emergency responder and not others? There could be several factors involved. Tragedy calls that involve children generally have the most impact, especially if the firefighter/EMT has a child the same age or the same build. It is also difficult if the victim reminds one of a spouse, a parent, or another loved one, or is someone the responder knows personally.

Tragedies involving fellow firefighters impact the responders at two levels. Not only do the responders lose a comrade, but they also face a stark reminder that no one is invincible, even those who must behave every day as if they are. Much attention is given in the fire service to fire-ground safety, but all firefighters know that any shift they work, any call they run, could require them to make the ultimate sacrifice to save a life. Something as simple as a small garage fire could prove fatal if there are multiple cans of gun powder or large rocket engines stored in the garage. (Both of these situations have happened on calls in my community.) The dangers abound.

We train constantly and seek to be as safe as possible in fighting fires, but the hidden, unforeseen dangers that can take life put untold amounts of stress on these heroes.

Sometimes a call run many times with no visible effects will serve as the straw that breaks the camel's back. These are the silent killers—no noticeable signs until one day it hits and the responder is gone. Or multiple difficult calls close together might send someone over the edge. Smells, sights, sounds, or tactile sensations that evoke previous traumatic calls can trigger anxiety and post-traumatic stress. Every person is different. The key is to get the conversation started and remove the stigma that often comes with reaching out for help.

A fire chief in the Dallas area recently reached out to me about one of his best firefighter/paramedics. The young man had turned in his resignation and was looking for another career. He'd been with the department for several years and was good at what he did. He had a heart to serve others and had paid his own way through the fire academy and paramedic school. The chief asked him if he would be willing to visit with me. He agreed.

We met for four hours on his first visit. He unloaded a world of hurt. I learned that several weeks earlier he had run an especially difficult pediatric call. The child was deceased when he arrived; he could not revive him. The screams and wails of family members, along with overwhelming feelings of helplessness and worthlessness, began to eat at him. He continued pulling his shifts and running calls, but he would wake up with night sweats, picturing the mother holding the lifeless body of her child while she wailed and uttered gibberish through her sobs.

Over the next few weeks, he ran two other tragic calls involving a young child and a teenager. He got to the point where he couldn't sleep. When the alarm would go off at the station, he would nearly jump out of his skin, start sweating profusely, and have anxiety attacks. Somehow, he managed to suck it up and do what he was trained to do when they arrived at the scene.

This firefighter had the presence of mind to know that he did not need to be running fire or medical calls in his current state and decided to pull himself out of the game. He assumed it would be the end of his career. In this business, the standard rhetoric about those who drop out is that they were never cut out to be firefighters in the first place.

I learned that this man was a believer, and we began to use his faith to reframe the original call that had plagued him. As he sat there with the family, not knowing what to say or do, he began to hear in his mind, "What are you even doing here?" "See, you don't make a difference." "You are worthless." I asked him if he believed that the messages he was telling himself were from heaven or from hell. He agreed that Satan, the accuser, the enemy of all that is good, had been the originator of the messages. We sat together as he listened for what the Lord, the Great Physician, who had also been in the room with them, had to say. He had other messages: "You are My child." "I appointed you to this place at this time to be My presence of calm." "You don't have to know what to say, just be My calming presence." "You are doing exactly what I am calling you to do in this moment."

As his perception of the event changed, so did his demeanor. We spent time in prayer where he was given permission to vent to God—unfiltered—about all that he had experienced and how he was feeling about the event, himself, and God. I assured him that God could take anything he had to say. As we wept and embraced, this tough firefighter began to see himself and his calling in a new light. Over the next several weeks, we addressed some other issues, and he began to heal.

Three months after our first visit, he told me that the chief had said he could return to work if I cleared him. I am not a mental healthcare professional, but Champion Responders partners with a trauma specialist counselor, who is a believer. He is available to help with any emergency responders who come to me for help. I can address the spiritual aspects, which are huge, while he can address the psychological issues. After a three-hour visit in my office, the counselor and I cleared the young man to go back to work with his department. I am happy to say that after several months, he is doing well and serving his community. He has the tools now to put his experiences in a healthier place and do the necessary work to de-stress when faced with a traumatic call.

I'm even more thrilled with the larger impact this situation had. I learned later from his chief that his coming forward with his critical incident stress was the best thing that had happened to their department. Even the old-timers rallied around him and began sharing their own stories of traumatic calls that still affected them. For the first time, they all began to get relief. The younger firefighter no longer felt alone. No one cast him out. Instead, an open and honest dialogue regarding traumatic calls began within that department. The chief later expressed his gratitude for the culture change that came about as a result of the incident. He believes this new paradigm will serve them well as the department grows.

Deconstructing the Story

My *In for the Long Haul* training is designed to give tools like these to entire fire departments and to start the discussion of critical incident stress management. Everything I do with firefighters and their families is at no cost to them. Firefighters and emergency responders come from all over the Dallas-Fort Worth metroplex seeking help with traumatic stress, post-traumatic stress disorder, marital difficulties, substance abuse, and general life issues. Ultimately, they need an intimate relationship with the Great Physician, Jesus Christ. While as a chaplain, I can't begin discussing that relationship unless I am invited to do so, there hasn't been anyone yet who has not opened the door to share the message of hope from Jesus.

Often, I've learned, the responders are not traumatized by the events themselves, but rather by their unique perception or interpretation of the events and the meanings and beliefs they've attached to those interpretations. In other words, the *story* they tell themselves about the event impacts their worldview from that point forward.

The key is to take apart those initial perceptions, the meanings, the beliefs, and the story. Often, these are based on information that is not even true. That is why a Critical Incident Stress Debrief can be so helpful in filling in the gaps of the events. For example, a firefighter/medic may be impacted by regret after a fatality, thinking they had missed a critical step. When he learns that another medic had already taken that step before he reached the patient, his perception of the story changes.

The Problem of Suffering

Suffering and pain demand answers. "Why do undeserved bad things happen to good people?" While everyone struggles to make sense of tragedy and pain, the question is a common refrain in the minds of emergency workers. Hundreds, perhaps thousands, of books have been written on this subject, but after years of wrestling with this dilemma myself, I take a simple approach: *because we live in a fallen world consumed with sin, darkness, and evil.*

Adam and Eve disobeyed God in the special place He had prepared for humankind, the Garden of Eden. Their rejection of God and His provision opened a Pandora's box of sorts. It brought pain, suffering, disease, death, injustice, trauma, and evil into the world in which we live. The ruler, or "god of this world," as Jesus calls him (John 12:31), is ruthless in his desire to steal, kill, and destroy (John 10:10). He often shrouds his cunning devices in things that have the appearance of bringing pleasure, satisfaction, and happiness.

In the wake of trauma or extreme crisis, we wail, "Why?" "Why this?" "Why now?" "Why me?" "Why my family?" Jesus cried out the same word as He hung on the cross for the sins of the world: "Why?" (Matt. 27:46). It wasn't time for an intellectual conversation. He knew why. But in His humanness and in His pain, He cried it out anyway.

It's *Not* All God's Will

I'm going to go out on a limb here and share something that I know many might take issue with regarding the sovereignty of God. I simply ask that you hear me out before drawing any conclusions. I will do my best to explain my understanding of it based on Scripture. Here it is: *I do not believe that everything that happens is God's will.*

Was it God's will for a beautiful, six-year-old girl to be brutally raped, murdered, rolled up in a tarp, and left in the middle of the street, as the firefighter/paramedic who was first on the scene and unrolled the tarp described to me? I don't know how many times I've heard someone say, "If [fill in the blank] is God's will, then I don't want to have anything to do with Him." We soften this misunderstanding with statements like "God wanted to take him or her" or "God needed another star in the sky." The question is: Does everything that happens happen because God wills it to happen?

Second Peter 3:9 says that God is "*not willing* that any should perish but that all should come to repentance." What is he saying? It is the will of God that everyone be saved, that all come to repentance and faith in Jesus Christ and have eternal life with Him. If this is true, then what are we to make of Jesus's teaching in the Sermon on the Mount in Matthew 7:13–14?

> Enter by the narrow gate; for wide is the gate and broad is the way that leads to destruction, and there are many who go in by it. Because narrow is the gate and difficult is the way which leads to life, and there are few who find it.

I could be wrong, but this verse seems to teach that most people will not repent, follow Christ, and be saved. Most people will reject His love, His grace, and His gift of salvation and will be lost to everlasting destruction. Those who choose everlasting life will be relatively few.

So I ask again, does God always get His will? While He may allow the natural consequences of humankind's living in a sinful and fallen world to unfold, thus causing undeserved suffering to many who are innocent, the Scriptures also tell us that sin and its consequences grieve Him.

The Presence in the Midst of Pain

Without question, there have been times that God has intervened and brought about miraculous healing and protection from loss, but when and why He chooses to do so is not within the realm of our understanding. Isaiah 55:8–9 tells us that His thoughts and ways are higher than our ability to comprehend. This mystery can frustrate believers who suffer tragedy or loss, especially if they've seen Him intervene in the lives of others. It's hard for parents who lose their child to tragedy or who grieve because they can't have children of their own to see others who are seemingly less deserving have children they don't even want.

Jesus Christ came to redeem our brokenness, our fallenness, our hurts, our pain, and our loss. John 10:10–11 says:

> The thief does not come except to steal, and to kill, and to destroy. I have come that they may have life, and that they may have it more abundantly. I am the good shepherd. The good shepherd gives His life for the sheep.

God does not promise believers that they will be exempt from trials, tragedy, and loss. In fact, He tells us that we may suffer more because we are believers (2 Tim. 3:12; 2 Cor. 4:8–9). Read *Foxe's Book of Martyrs*, or listen to the news reports about the brutal violence targeted at Christians. But regardless of what happens to us in this life, Jesus promises, "I will be with you always" (Matt. 28:20).

Not only is He our God and Savior, but He is our perfect High Priest who personally understands suffering, rejection, trauma, tragedy, and loss. Thus we can come with confidence to His throne to find grace and mercy to help in time of need (Heb. 4:15–16). It is in our suffering—or in being present in the suffering of others—that we are often surprised to feel His presence more strongly than at any other time. And many times, He demonstrates His care and love through the compassion of His people.

Steve Calvert

Community of Chaplains

An important aspect of the our ministry is the passion that God has laid on my heart to work with the Texas Corps of Fire Chaplains and the Federation of Fire Chaplains: to come along side those in the midst of tragedy and minister the love and compassion of Jesus Christ. When disaster strikes, these are the men and women whom those running the disaster response want to see coming. We are currently creating a model for building local networks of mutual aid chaplains from surrounding cities to work together in being effective ambassadors for Christ and crisis intervention. We want to be agents of redemption.

We recently implemented this model when we had a flood in Coppell that displaced more than five hundred families. The city worked together with the Red Cross to set up a shelter, and I was asked by the city to run the relief efforts on the ground for the victims. The Red Cross provided cots for the shelter and some food. God brought together many believers who banded together to provide everything else. We gathered more than $15,000 in gift cards and distributed most of them directly to the victims who had lost their homes. We filled a local church gymnasium with everything from clothes and shoes to hardware, food, household items, etc. I called fire chaplains from surrounding cities to come and help minister to those in need; even more chaplains were on standby. It was a tremendous collaborative effort, the first of its kind in our community. I heard from those in the Red Cross and another international disaster relief organization that they had never before seen the kind of personal love, care, and attention given to victims—or the outpouring of love and gratitude of the victims toward the caregivers—that they'd seen in Coppell.

Champion Responders

We are excited to share that, as of August 2015, Champion Responders is officially its own 501(c)(3) non-profit corporation. We continue to raise funding toward our goal of providing more resources to firefighters, fire/police/EMS departments, and the emergency response industry. I am currently working to get the *In for the Long Haul* training course into book form.

My wife, Gina, is currently the senior content writer for the marketing department of a technology firm that produces church management software used by many of the largest churches in the nation. She led the thought leadership forum for the company, pouring into and helping to equip senior pastors and their ministry staffs throughout the nation. She is a gifted writer who has published a book on spiritual transformation and has spoken at numerous women's events. Now, Gina and I are creating a training program and book for married couples called *Together for the Long Haul.*

As the Lord continues to draw prayer and financial partners who have a heart for what the Lord is doing in the emergency response world, my goal is to bring Gina on board full time. She is eager to minister to women associated with fire service and contribute to our work with the level of professionalism she's brought to the corporate world and to thirty years of church ministry. We want to offer our help and support to firefighters and their families for free, as a ministry of grace and power.

By What Authority?

From the very beginning of the Champion Responders ministry, it has been my conviction that God is raising up an army of believers in the fire service and, remarkably, is using me, a cracked pot and broken vessel, as a leader in that effort. The whole industry is more open to learning about the spiritual aspects of their challenges with than it ever has been before. More and more departments nationwide that have never had a chaplaincy program—or that have previously been opposed to the idea—are inquiring about starting one.

Who can be a chaplain? Chaplains could be local pastors who have a heart for ministry to emergency responders and victims in their communities. They bring their deep faith; we connect them to training in critical incident stress management, trauma counseling and incident command (a critical need when working a major disaster). Chaplains from this background must be wary of saying or doing certain things that can alienate people in traumatic environments, even though they may work well in other situations. These chaplains must also learn to connect with firefighter/EMS personnel in their environment, "becom[ing] all things to all men" (1 Cor. 9:22). While chaplains may not think or talk the way the responders do, they can be with them as they are, encouraging, supporting, and offering guidance and direction.

Other chaplains may come from within the fire service itself: members of the department, possibly even officers, who are strong believers and want to use their callings and gifts to strengthen the faith of believers and demonstrate the abundant life to non-believers. These chaplains bring an awareness and familiarity of the culture of the fire service and they know how things operate at a fire scene. As we raise up and pour into fire department chaplains, they in turn minister to, strengthen, encourage, and equip believing warriors in their departments as well as those in crisis. The International Federation of Fire Chaplains (founded by Ed Stauffer, a retired firefighter and chaplain with the Fort Worth Fire Department) along with the Texas Corps of Fire Chaplains and other Federation Chapters throughout the nation are all dedicated to this same goal.

The Lord is moving among the world of emergency firefighters/EMTs and other emergency responders, gathering believers to serve on the front lines of whatever our country is about to face. Whatever that may be, emergency responders will be—and already are—the first to face the trauma and carnage that evil produces. To that end, God-fearing chaplains are being raised up to lead this offense against the enemy on the front lines. While our goal is to encourage, we must ask, "If this is spiritual warfare in its truest form, do our responders have the authority and spiritual armor they need to combat what they face with each call?"

Taking part in God's great work of equipping emergency responders with that authority is what Champion Responders is all about. This is spiritual warfare in its purest form. Will you join and support this battle?

Discussion Questions

1. What crisis in your own life have you faced that resulted in you crying out to God, "Why"?
2. How have you developed mental/spiritual resiliency in your own life or how have you seen it modeled in others?
3. What role do you think firefighters and other emergency responders will play in dealing with traumatic events as the current events in our nation unfold, if things continue on the path they are on?
4. How is God calling you personally to be a part of, or support, the front-line troops, firefighters, and emergency responders against the enemy seeking to destroy the people we love and our nation?

Resources for Further Study

Books

C. S. Lewis, *A Grief Observed* (San Francisco: HarperOne, 2009).
Norman Wright, *The Complete Guide to Crisis and Trauma Counseling,* rev. ed. (Bloomington, MN: Bethany House, 2011).
———. *Recovering from the Losses of Life,* rev. ed. (Grand Rapids: Revell, 2006).

Websites

Champion Responders, www.championresponders.com.
Federation of Fire Chaplains, firechaplains.org.
Texas Corps of Fire Chaplains, www.txcfc.org.

SIX

Redeeming the Loss of a Spouse:
God's Crucible of Affliction

RICK ROOD

Blessed be the Lord, who daily bears our burden, The God who is our salvation. (Ps. 68:19)[1]

The fact of suffering undoubtedly constitutes the single greatest challenge to the Christian faith."[2] These were the words of the late John Stott—and they are true.

Indeed, suffering does constitute a challenge to faith, both for the skeptic as well as for the believing Christian. For the skeptic, suffering poses a barrier to faith. "How can belief in a good and powerful God be reconciled with a world of evil and suffering?" For the believer, however, suffering poses a test of faith. "If God loves me, why has He allowed me to suffer in the ways I have?" It's in the crucible of affliction that our faith is tested. But it's also in the crucible of affliction that God's faithfulness is proven.

In the fall of 1984 my wife and I entered into the crucible of affliction in a way we never thought to endure.[3] I will never forget the day I was sitting in my office at Dallas Theological Seminary when my phone rang. It was my wife Polly. "The doctor just called," she said. Then in a slightly broken

---

1 All Scripture quotations are from the NASB.

2 John R. W. Stott, *The Cross of Christ* (Downers Grove, IL: InterVarsity Press, 1986), 311.

3 This chapter is adapted from my book *Our Story . . . His Story: One Couple's Encounter with Grace in the Crucible of Affliction* (Maitland, FL: Xulon, 2014).

voice, she continued, "He says he's 99 percent sure I do have the illness." I told our secretary that I had some urgent concerns to tend to at home, and I immediately left to spend the rest of the day with Polly. On the way home I recalled the first conversation she and I had ever had about the possibility that what we were told today might occur.

Polly and I met during our student days at Seattle Pacific University in the late 1960s; we served together in student government our junior year. There was something special about Polly. She was about 5'4" with faintly visible freckles and a contagious smile. She had chosen Seattle Pacific hoping to major in music, but she was humble enough to tell me that her professor had informed her that she likely would not excel in that field. So she decided to major in elementary education with a minor in history.

She also had a heart for ministry, having served the previous summer as part of a mission team putting on camps for Native American youth in British Columbia. I will never forget seeing her kneeling in prayer one evening with a classmate in the student body office. This told me something about her that nothing else quite could.

Over the course of the year, working together day in and day out, we gradually became attached to each other. I think there was something in me that wanted to guard and protect her. One evening while we were talking, she said to me, "Rick, you might as well know now. There's a 50 percent chance I might someday have Huntington's disease. My father died from the illness a couple of years ago." I respected her for telling me this. I had never heard of Huntington's disease (HD) before.

When I looked it up in the library the next day, I was sobered by what I read. Like most neurodegenerative illnesses, HD is a serious and debilitating disease. While onset of the illness occurs early in life for some, for most it begins later. The children of those affected by HD have a 50 percent chance of having the illness, but also a 50 percent chance of *not* having it. Though a genetic test was developed in the mid-1990s, at the time when Polly and I met there was no way to know if you had inherited it. You just waited to see. Polly's father and mother had parted ways when she was about 8 years old, and she did not see him again until she represented her family at his funeral in Oklahoma City. She had been sheltered from knowing about her father's disease until her junior year in high school.

Not long after Polly told me about her family history, her younger brother Chris began showing signs of HD. At 14 years old, Chris was a sweet boy with his sister's smile. He loved to shoot baskets with me outside their home in Philomath, Oregon, when I would go to visit them. We had read that there may be a tendency for children of males with HD to come down with the illness earlier in life. I think the fact that this was what was happening to Chris but not to Polly gave us hopes that she may have escaped it.

The prospect of Polly's having HD someday was a serious concern to me at that time. Yet I also found my love for her growing. I shared these concerns with my mother one day. She said to me, "Rick, none of us knows what we might have someday." When she met Polly, she told me, "Polly really is for you." Likewise, my pastor, whom I had come to love and respect as an insightful Bible teacher and who loved us both, was very encouraging with regard to our relationship.

Our wedding day, September 11, 1971, was a wonderful event. There have probably been countless weddings in that little country church in Blodgett, Oregon, but likely none quite like this one. The church was packed with family and friends from Seattle to San Francisco. Polly had prayed for a sunny day. And indeed it was—in more ways than one.

After graduating from Seattle Pacific, we journeyed across the country to Dallas, Texas, where for the next four years I attended Dallas Theological Seminary (DTS). Those were stressful years in some ways. But they were good years. Not only did the Lord provide us with the foundation for a lifetime of ministry, but we made many lifelong friends.

After I graduated from DTS, we returned to the Pacific Northwest, where I served as pastor to a fledgling congregation in the Seattle area. Those dear people exercised more patience with their freshman pastor than they probably ever anticipated they would need to. Among those who encouraged me was a couple by the name of Bill and Dorothea Hart. Bill had been diagnosed with Parkinson's disease early in their marriage; Dorothea had devoted herself to caring for him the remainder of his days. They showed us what faithfulness and love look like.

During the years of pastoring, however, I developed a desire to return to DTS for doctoral studies, with the hopes of teaching in a college or seminary someday. The Lord not only opened the door into the doctoral program, but also provided a place on the faculty in the Field Education Department.

In the summer of 1981, we made our way back to Dallas and began a new chapter of our life. A few years later we moved into a new home and discovered that our neighbors across the street, Al and Jeane Olson, were a couple who had served as missionaries in Guatemala. Al had been diagnosed with an unusual neurodegenerative illness early in their marriage. As a result, they had returned from the mission field so he could receive the care that he needed, while his wife Jeane worked in the mission office in Dallas. It would soon become apparent to us why the Lord had led us to settle across the street from Al and Jeane, just as He had led Bill and Dorothea Hart to our congregation years before. I will be forever grateful for the love and example of these two dear couples.

The previous summer, Polly had spent a couple weeks' vacation with her family in Oregon. At the end of the summer we attended a family reunion of Polly's loved ones in DeQueen, Arkansas, where Polly's grandmother resided. While there, Polly's stepfather took me aside, and said, "Rick, while Polly was visiting with us we noticed some changes in her. We think you should take her to see a doctor. We believe she's showing signs of HD." I don't know what my first response was, but I'm sure there was more than a tinge of disbelief. It was the last thing that I wanted to hear at that time.

When I first took Polly to see a neurologist in Dallas, he told us that he didn't see any signs of HD in her. But a year later, when she saw him again, he noticed things that caused some concern. We went back for a full day of tests. I remember seeing her wistfully looking out the window while we were waiting for her to be called for one of the tests. I wondered what she was thinking, but I really didn't need to ask. It was a week or so later that Polly called to tell me the test results.

When we first learned of Polly's diagnosis, we still were in somewhat of a state of denial. While I didn't doubt the results of the test, I thought of every other possible reason why she might be showing these symptoms—her occasional problems with balance, her slight awkwardness, and her small involuntary movements. I was hoping that these were all just signs of stress. Years later I would become chaplain in two hospitals in Dallas, where I would see many patients who were in denial about their diagnosis. I learned that denial is normal. It actually helps us cope, protecting us from being overwhelmed by a painful reality—at least for a while.

It wasn't long, however, before denial was replaced by a flood of emotions. Feelings of fear about the future and of protest about what this diagnosis meant for our lives. We couldn't sleep at night; we struggled to make decisions. Though we kept going through our daily routine, the joy of living had faded. We began to realize all the losses that would follow in the wake of this unwelcome intruder into our life, and we grieved.

A few weeks after Polly's diagnosis, I believe, I was again sitting in my office at DTS early in the morning. It had been my practice to begin my work day by reading a passage of Scripture; at this time I was reading through the Psalms. My eyes fell on Psalm 55:22: "Cast your burden upon the LORD and He will sustain you; He will never allow the righteous to be shaken." I noticed a footnote that told me the word "burden" could be rendered "what He has given you." It was as though the Lord was speaking directly to me, letting me know that what was happening to us was not outside the scope of His gracious purposes for us.

A few days later I read Psalm 68:19, "Blessed be the LORD, who daily bears our burden, the God who is our salvation." I cannot tell you what these two verses meant to me at that time. I believe the Lord used these verses to let me know that He could be trusted with our future. It was as though He was saying to us, "Lean on Me. I will carry you throughout the rest of your life, one day at a time. I will not let you down." Even still, there are tears in my eyes as I remember the hope these verses instilled in my heart that day. It was exactly what I needed to know.

The next several years saw many adjustments in our life. For one, there was the adjustment of living with a wife who was gradually becoming someone different from the girl I married. Though she never lost her sweet spirit, she slowly lost her ability to do so many things—to drive, walk, dress and bathe herself, feed herself, remember everything she wanted to, speak, eat. As we grieved the loss of normalcy, we also grieved the loss of hopes and dreams. Due to the increase in responsibilities at home, I eventually had to relinquish my dream of finishing my doctoral studies at DTS, with only the dissertation remaining to be completed.

We also went through adjustments in our relationships with friends and others outside our family. Even though most of our friends knew that Polly had HD, it wasn't always possible for them to understand exactly what to expect of her. This lack of understanding sometimes put a strain on our relationships with others. Of course, most people were very kind and wanted to be helpful and understanding.

But occasionally someone would make a remark that wasn't exactly helpful. A week after Polly's diagnosis, for example, someone called Polly at home and told her that she was confident that if Polly had faith, God would heal her completely. A few people suggested that if we had real faith, we would take Polly off her medications and just trust God to heal her. Another person inquired as to whether there might be some sin behind Polly's illness. Yet another simply urged us to accept HD as God's will for our life. Encounters such as these tended to create some distance between us and others. It just seemed safer to withdraw and avoid such exchanges. This led to a degree of self-imposed isolation.

One day in the spring of 1992, we were in our living room when Polly said to me, "Rick, I think it's time I move into a nursing home." We had contemplated this possibility before, but we had avoided discussing it for some time. I remember asking her doctor when he thought it would be appropriate for us to consider this. He said, "Well, you'll just know. You won't be able to do everything that needs to be done." We both realized that we had reached that place. With all the responsibilities of caregiving on top of working full time and caring for our children, it was all we could do just to survive. When I began visiting local nursing homes, I could hardly envision Polly residing there. She was just 41 years old; it seemed like everyone there was twice her age or more. One of our neighbors, however, who was a nurse, recommended a nursing home in the Pleasant Grove area of Dallas. When I visited this facility, I could see why she had suggested it. Many of the residents were even younger than Polly.

I will never forget the day I first brought Polly to the nursing home. As we passed by the nurses' station in the middle of the home, she smiled and said, "Hi. I'm Polly. I'm new." I could tell the staff was glad to have her. She was assigned to a room of about 10 x 15 feet, with a small bathroom, a closet, and a dresser. Her roommate, an elderly lady, had been there for some time. I placed her clothing in the dresser and hung some in her closet. Then I walked with her down to the dining hall to stay with her for lunch.

As I looked around the room I realized that we had entered a very different world from anything we had known before. Some of the residents were drooling. Some were mumbling to themselves. Others were just quietly sitting, waiting for their meal to be served. One table was reserved for people who needed to have their meals fed to them. That would become Polly's table, too. I wondered if we would ever adjust to being part of this world. I can tell you though, that over time we came to love the nursing home life. For the most part, the people who resided there had been reduced to their basic human essence. They had nothing to prove and nothing to lose. I miss it now very much.

When I left the nursing home that day, I stopped to look back at what I realized would be my wife's home for the rest of her life. I had a mixture of gratitude and grief. Gratitude that she would now have much more assistance than I could possibly provide alone. But also grief that she had come to need this much care.

For the first couple of weeks, I visited Polly every other night and brought her home on the weekends. But the social worker told me that Polly seemed depressed on the nights I was not there. So I resolved to see her every night. After making dinner for our children and helping them get started on their homework, I drove to the nursing home to spend an hour or more with Polly.

We would walk down to the dining room where I would get her a glass of iced tea to drink, or we would go outside where we could sit on a bench under a tree. We would talk about our day and pray together. We prayed especially for our children, whom we loved very much.

Nursing home life can be a bit mundane in certain respects. Every day is pretty much the same. But the staff usually tries hard to make life interesting and bring some joy to those who live there. One of the events that Polly enjoyed was "balloon volleyball." You can imagine what this was like. Part of the dining room would be cleared of the tables and chairs, and the two opposing teams of wheelchair-bound residents would have the greatest time batting a balloon back and forth across the room. It was great fun.

There were also special occasions such as Christmas and Thanksgiving when the staff would prepare a special dinner for residents and their families. I would bring one of Polly's nicest dresses, and we would slowly walk down to the dining room to enjoy the evening. Usually there was also special entertainment, such as a band or a singing group from the community. These were great times, and they forged many memories for us.

I realized as well that it was important to get Polly out of the nursing home as often as possible. So I planned outings a couple of times per week. Concerts, movies, sporting events, trips to a park—these were just some of the things we enjoyed for many years. I think we attended every football and basketball game at our kids' high school during their student years, and even for a while after. Sunday mornings we would attend church, sitting at the back of the congregation—Polly in her wheelchair, and me next to her. I remember Polly looking at me one day and saying, "Rick, you help make my life worthwhile." Knowing that meant the world to me.

About four years after Polly entered the nursing home, I was able to move her to a new home that had just opened on the shores of Lake Ray Hubbard, just east of Dallas. It wasn't long before I realized what a blessing this would prove to be. One Saturday I planned to take her to a Greek Orthodox church to see the beautiful artwork inside. But as I tried to wheel her into the building, her body kept wanting to exit the wheelchair. I never was able to get her inside.

As I drove her back to the nursing home I said to myself, "This is probably the last time I will ever be able to take Polly out." It was. For about the last four years of her life, she was removed from her bed only to be taken for a bath or to the hospital. No longer could I take her to places she could enjoy; now it became a matter of bringing some joy to her bedside. In years past, I had enjoyed taking her to concerts; now I played worship music at her bedside.

It seemed also that our focus began to turn toward heaven and to the hopes that lie beyond this world and this life. I recall one day playing a song to her that spoke of our hope of heaven, when life's trials will be only a faint memory from the past. She had not been able to speak for some time now. I wondered if she was listening. A tear, silently streaming down her cheek told me that she was. I remember as well an occasion a few years before this when I was reading to her Paul's letter to the Philippians. It seemed to me that Polly was dozing off to sleep, but when I got to the part in the first chapter where Paul writes that to be with Christ is "better by far," she opened her eyes, lifted up her head, and said to me, "I know that." She then resumed her restful pose.

A couple of years later, the doctors discovered that Polly had breast cancer. She received a radical mastectomy, after which her doctor put her on tamoxifen. When I asked if he recommended any more aggressive treatment, he said, "No. In light of her overall health condition I really do not."

The last few years of Polly's life were really years of waiting. Polly's life had become increasingly confined—and so had mine. I remember driving on the freeway one day and talking to the Lord about what His purposes could be for our lives. I realized that Polly could linger in this condition for quite some time. I remember praying, "Lord, I don't understand the purpose of our lives right now. But if You can be most glorified by my remaining by her bedside for as long as You choose, until You take her home, I'm willing."

If someone were to ask if I ever considered leaving Polly, I can honestly say that I never did. Though our married life had turned out to be anything but what we had expected and hoped for, our marriage bond was sacred. I'm well aware that some marriages do suffer a mortal wound. But this had not happened to us. I was prepared to stay by Polly until the Lord took her home, however long that might be.

Someone has said that if all it took for marriage to succeed is to "do what comes naturally," then there would be no need to consecrate marriage with a vow.[4] Marriage requires of us what does *not* come naturally. And because it does, it also requires faith—faith that God will provide all we need to not only remain true to our vows, but to use our marriage to further His own work in our hearts.

It was during these days that I began to reflect more seriously on what God had been doing in our lives all these years. It had been more than fifteen

---

4 These thoughts on vows in marriage were inspired by Mike Mason, *The Mystery of Marriage* (Portland: Multnomah, 1984), 91–110.

years since He had spoken to me through those two psalms as I sat in my office that morning in 1984.

During these years I had also noted how often the Bible mentions that when God's people pass through times of affliction, He is with them in a special way. When Joseph was in slavery and then in prison, the text says, "But the LORD was with Joseph" (Gen. 39:21). When the apostle Paul stood trial before Nero, he wrote to Timothy, "At my first defense no one supported me but all deserted me. . . . But the Lord stood with me and strengthened me" (2 Tim. 4:16–17a). When Israel was in exile, the Lord said to the nation, "Do not fear, for I am with you; do not anxiously look about you, for I am your God, I will strengthen you, surely I will help you, Surely I will uphold you with My righteous right hand" (Isa. 41:10).

Over these years I had been keeping a journal in which I recorded many of the things I saw the Lord doing in our lives. I've already noted how the Lord had obviously exposed us to the loving example of the two dear couples whom He placed in our lives—Bill and Dorothea Hart in Seattle, and Al and Jeane Olson in Texas. When it came time for Polly to move into the nursing home, the Lord's hand was again with us in a special way. Nursing home care is not cheap; the only way we could afford such care was through Medicaid assistance. For Polly to qualify for Medicaid, she needed to be declared disabled (which she was), and our total assets needed to fall under the cap established by the state. I believe we fell under the cap by just a few hundred dollars. A month later I realized that if we had waited just one more month, our assets would have gone over the cap, and we would have been denied coverage for the following two years. I don't know how we would have survived those two years if she had not received Medicaid assistance when she did. I had often wondered why the Lord kept our income quite so lean during those years. But now I understood at least one reason He had.

During the first few years Polly resided in the nursing home, I was serving as director of publications for Probe Ministries, a Christian apologetics and educational ministry in the Dallas area. These were years when we were adjusting to the serious challenges of our lives, and it was easy to grow discouraged.

One day at the Probe office, a colleague of mine entered my office and handed me a book that had come in the mail. The authors had sent this book to us in hopes of our marketing it to our constituency. This is the only request of this nature I remember receiving during the years that I served at Probe. When I looked at the book I could tell that it was not the kind of book that would likely appeal to many of the people we served. It was the life story of a married couple. But when I opened the book, I realized that this was the story of a couple affected by the same rare illness Polly had—Huntington's disease. The authors did not know me or anything about Polly. Why they sent it to us, I did not know. But I believe I know why the Lord directed them to send it to us—as a means of encouragement to us. And indeed it was.

During these years we learned to live on a tight budget. This was not always easy, especially when our son and daughter were teenagers. When our son was in junior high school I noticed that he rarely smiled. It didn't take long for me to learn why: he had a gap between his upper front teeth. No doubt some of his peers had frequently reminded him of it; he was very self-conscious about it. I wanted to do something for him, but I also knew that orthodontic work does not come cheap. I learned that the total cost for braces for his teeth was in excess of $3,000—a considerable sum for us at the time. So I prayed about it. I wanted to help him, but I didn't want to take on more financial burdens than we could bear. So I prayed, "Lord, if You want me to do this for him, show me in some way that You intend to provide for it."

I decided to make an appointment for the initial exam, which cost $270. On that very day I discovered three envelopes in our mailbox. One contained a check for $10 from a friend, in payment for our driving their child to school in the mornings. The other two envelopes came from friends across the country who knew nothing of our current needs. One of them contained a check for $60, and the third contained a check for $200. The total of the three checks was exactly $270. Need I say anything more? Our son got his braces, and his smile gradually returned.

On another occasion near this time our car broke down at the end of our street. It was completely undrivable. The following day we received a $1,000 gift from an anonymous donor who knew nothing about our situation.

I am not suggesting that we should just sit back and expect God to fill our mailbox with checks. He normally uses our work as well as our frugality. But everything we have ultimately comes from Him; and there are times when He reminds us of this fact, sometimes in extraordinary ways. These were two examples of such times; and they were an immense encouragement to us.

I think it was less than a year after Polly entered the nursing home near Lake Ray Hubbard that it became apparent that she was having a hard time swallowing her food. The nursing home staff sent her to the hospital for some tests, after which it was suggested that she consider going on a feeding tube. The social worker asked us to take a couple of days to think it over. It was a decision only Polly could make, but I wanted to be the best encouragement to her I could be. I was serving at the time as a full-time chaplain at a hospital in the Dallas area. While making my rounds the morning after our conversation about the feeding tube, I met a female patient and her husband sitting in the chair next to her. As we talked, I learned that she was in the hospital to receive a permanent feeding tube. What surprised me, though, was that she had Huntington's disease—Polly's illness. I only see hospital patients with HD once every year or two. But I saw her on the very day I needed some encouragement regarding Polly's decision. More than a mere coincidence.

I could multiply examples like these. But these are enough to illustrate the many things that God did *for* us, guiding and providing during the course of Polly's illness. It's in the crucible of affliction that our faith is tested; but it's also in the crucible of affliction that God's faithfulness is proven. This is something we learned by experience during Polly's long journey.

Not only was God at work *for* us, but He was also at work *in* us. Affliction has a way of forcing us to deal with our hearts, and I knew He was at work reshaping and molding my heart through all that we were experiencing. A couple weeks after Polly's death, my daughter and I were walking in our nearby mall over the lunch hour. She said to me, "Dad, I think the reason God put you with Mom was because He knew you had the qualities necessary to care for her." Well, I know my own heart better than she does. I said to her, "You know, I think one reason God put me with your mom is because He knew I needed to *acquire* the qualities needed to care for her."

I well remember the day in the summer of 1990 when it occurred to me in a new way how much Polly's illness was affecting her. I had always loved her; I never raised my voice at her. Yet as the illness progressed and the stresses of caregiving increased, it was not always easy to be patient with her. I had naturally been focused on how much her illness had affected my life—and it had. My life was turned upside down by what happened to Polly. But I realized in that moment that how her illness was affecting my life paled in comparison to how it was affecting *her* life. I remember praying, "Lord, help me never to say an impatient word to Polly again." For the remainder of her days, by God's grace, I don't believe I ever did. I loved Polly when I married her. But years later when I laid her to rest, I had learned to love her in a much deeper way. Scripture tells us that there are three qualities above all that the Lord is seeking to instill in us: "faith, hope, and love . . . but the greatest of these is love" (1 Cor. 13:13).

Not only was God at work *for* us and *in* us, but I had become aware that God was accomplishing His work *through* us. For all of my adult life I had been involved in full-time ministry as a pastor and a teacher. Yet in early 1996 I had come to a point where I wondered how, in light of our life situation, I could possibly continue in my current ministry. It was then, through a "chance" conversation with a friend, that the Lord directed my attention to hospital chaplaincy. I had never even considered this kind of ministry. Yet over the course of several months, it became apparent to me that the Lord had been preparing me for this all along. Since the fall of 1996, I've had the privilege of serving as chaplain at two hospitals in the Dallas area, an acute care hospital and a psychiatric hospital. I have no doubt that this was God's purpose for me, and that part of His preparation for this wonderful work took place during the years of caring for Polly. I will be forever grateful.

Early in the morning of July 24, 2003, I was listening to a Christian radio station as I prepared for my day. I walked across the room to sit down on our bed and read the day's selection from the devotional "Our Daily Bread."[5] As I reached over to turn off the radio, the spokesperson said, "What would you say to your loved one if you knew tomorrow would be their last day?" An interesting question. I opened the devotional for that day and read the title: "Say It Now!" You can understand how its title grabbed my attention, just after the comment on the radio a moment before. Part of the text of the devotional for that day reads as follows:

An unknown author has penned these thought-provoking words:

> I would rather have one little rose
>   From the garden of a friend
> Than to have the choicest flowers
>   When my stay on earth must end.

> I would rather have a pleasant word
>   In kindness said to me
> Than flattery when my heart is still,
>   And life has ceased to be.

> I would rather have a loving smile
>   From friends I know are true
> Than tears shed 'round my casket
>   When to this world I bid adieu.

---

5   "Our Daily Bread" is the devotional published by Our Daily Bread Ministries (formerly RBC Ministries), P.O. Box 2222, Grand Rapids, MI 49501-2222.

> Bring me all your flowers today,
>   Whether pink, or white, or red;
> I'd rather have one blossom now
>   Than a truckload when I'm dead.

Recalling the good qualities of deceased friends or relatives at their funeral is appropriate, but how much better to give sincere praise to them while they are still living. It may be the encouragement they desperately need. . . . Do you owe someone a word of thanks or appreciation? Don't put it off. Say it today. Tomorrow may be too late![6]

I realized that God was speaking to me. I resolved that when I went to see Polly that evening I would tell her how much I loved her.

That evening a friend dropped by Polly's room to leave her some flowers. It was the first and only time this friend had visited Polly. After she left, I took Polly to the shower room for her evening shower. When we finished, I stooped down to talk to her face to face. I said, "Polly, I just want you to know how much I love you and I want to thank you for all that you did for me and the kids during the years you were at home with us. We are so grateful for you. You have been an example to us through the years. I want you to know that there are hundreds of people all over the world who know about your life and are praying for you." Polly had been unable to speak for quite some time, but the look in her dark brown eyes as she stared directly at me spoke more than any words could say.

The following evening I was sitting in the sanctuary of a church at the funeral of a young man who had been in the ICU at the hospital where I was chaplain. During the service, I received a page. I recognized it as the number of Polly's nursing home. "Hello, Rick. This is Polly's nurse. She's having difficulty breathing, and we've sent her across the street to Lake Pointe Hospital. You need to meet her there in the ER as soon as you can." I immediately drove to the hospital, where I was greeted by the staff and directed to her room. She was barely conscious; the doctors had given her a breathing treatment and antibiotics. Soon they moved her to a room on the third floor.

This was not the first time she had been hospitalized for pneumonia, but it was definitely the hardest. For the next two weeks the staff did the best they could to help her recover, but the treatments just weren't enough this time. On

---

6 "Say It Now!" by Richard De Haan, in "Our Daily Bread," July 24, 2003 (Grand Rapids: RBC Ministries, 2003). Used with permission of Our Daily Bread Ministries.

August 5, I stopped by to see her during my lunch hour. She did not look well. I told the staff I would return as soon as I had fulfilled my obligation at the psych hospital where I served as part-time chaplain. On the way there, however, I received a call from Polly's nurse, telling me that she had gone into respiratory distress. I returned to the hospital. As I entered her room they were giving her morphine, which resulted in her slipping into a deep sleep.

A couple of hours later I asked her doctor what reasonable interventions we could take at this point. He said, "I could put her on the respirator, but she's so weak that she would never come off it." I knew that Polly would not want to live in that condition with no hope of recovery. There is a time to let go. This was Polly's time.

That evening our children and their spouses joined me around Polly's bed as we prayed for her and entrusted her to the Lord. At midnight I went home to get some rest.

The next morning I returned to Polly's room to find her alert and watching me as I moved about her room. I was surprised to find her so. At 8:43 am her nurse came in for her morning feeding through her tube. I stood across from her bed. At 8:45 am Polly quietly left her earthly tent and slipped into the presence of her Lord and Savior, and of all her loved ones who had gone before. Her long and unexpected journey had finally come to its earthly end.

I couldn't help but think of the unusual occurrence two weeks before when I heard the comment on the radio and had read "Our Daily Bread." Certainly, God knew that we needed this encouragement on the day before she would leave the nursing home for the very last time.

When I think back over Polly's life, the memories sometimes overwhelm me. But when I think of all that the Lord did *for* us as well as *in* us and *through* us during all those years, I must confess that I'm overwhelmed by the memories of His mercy and grace.

Soli Deo Gloria

Discussion Questions

1. Reflecting on unexpected affliction in your own life, how would you describe your own reaction to these events? Did you experience denial, shock, lament?
2. How has God encouraged you in the face of affliction in your life? What are some things that God has been doing *for* you in the midst of the affliction?

3. How has God been using affliction to accomplish His work *in* you? What changes have you been able to see in your own life that He has been bringing about through affliction?

4. How has God worked *through* you in the lives of others—or how might He do so in the future—as a result of your affliction?

Resources for Further Study

Books

Carol Dettoni, *Caring for Those Who Can't: Caregiving for Your Loved One—and Yourself* (Wheaton, IL: Victor, 1993).

Timothy Keller, *Walking with God through Pain and Suffering* (New York: Dutton, 2013).

John F. Kilner, Arlene B. Miller, and Edmund D. Pellegrino, eds. *Dignity and Dying: A Christian Appraisal* (Grand Rapids: Eerdmans, 1996).

June Cerza Kolf, *Comfort and Care for the Critically Ill* (Grand Rapids: Baker, 1993).

Charles Puchta, *Biblical Caregiving Principles: Scriptural Guidance on Caring for Aging or Ill Family Members.* 2nd ed. (Cincinnati: Aging America Resources, 2004).

———, *The Caregiver Resource Guide: Things You Need To Know Before You Know You Need Them.* Cincinnati: Aging America Resources, 2004-2005).

Rood, Rick. *Our Story . . . His Story: One Couple's Encounter with the Grace of God in the Crucible of Affliction* (Maitland, FL: Xulon, 2014).

Kay Marshall Strom, *A Caregiver's Survival Guide: How to Stay Healthy When Your Loved One Is Sick* (Downers Grove, IL: InterVarsity Press, 2000).

Websites

Aging America Resources Care Ministry. www.CareMinistry.com.
Huntington's Disease Society of America. www.hdsa.org.

SEVEN

Redeeming the Homeless:
One Man's Experience and Vision

WAYNE WALKER

> Since God chose you to be the holy people he loves, you must clothe yourselves with tenderhearted mercy, kindness, humility, gentleness, and patience. (Col. 3:12, NLT)[1]

D ysfunction" is not a dirty word. Every person struggles with it. Today I may be dysfunctional in the way I drive or when I spill coffee on my shirt. But some forms of dysfunction are disabling. They can limit our activity, our movement, keep us from operating at the level that we desire. For some, dysfunction may compound and increase exponentially until it enchains every area of their lives. They are stuck. They are suffering.

When I was only ten years old, my parents opened our home as an officially licensed foster home through the state of Texas. In total, sixty-seven different children stayed with us. Many came from homes of total dysfunction. Some had been tortured physically; the scars of others were hidden in deep emotional trauma. I heard them scream with nightmares. I listened to their stories of pain as we played together. I saw their suffering.

My past has truly been a blessing, though I wouldn't have seen that except by the grace of God. I never wanted to share my family or our home with foster kids. I never wanted to struggle with my own demons of addiction, depression, and suicidal feelings—but all of these were potholes on the road that led me to Christ, and for that I rejoice.

---

1 All Scripture quotations are from NIV unless otherwise indicated.

My family's ministry to foster care prepared me for my ministry. Today I am the founder, pastor, and executive director of a discipleship ministry that serves thousands of homeless individuals. What started out fifteen years ago as a group of volunteers handing out sandwiches on the downtown streets has grown into a full-time ministry that serves to meet the spiritual needs of a constantly growing population of homeless men, women, and children. We have met so many homeless friends that I could never remember all of their names or stories. In fact, we created a fairly sophisticated iPad app to record the details of almost 7,500 homeless friends. We record interactions, prayer requests, hospital and jail visits, and thousands of GPS coordinates where we visit homeless friends on their turf. Our teams trek under bridges, behind liquor stores, in abandoned buildings, in wooded encampments, on the outskirts of parks, and where cars are abandoned. We find people who are suffering and we reach out to them with the love of Christ. This is our calling, thus the name of our ministry: OurCalling. We incorporated as a 501(c)(3) in 2009; today we have ten employees working with an army of thousands of volunteers.

Four stories from the Gospels capture my thoughts as I think about suffering and dysfunction within the homeless community. In these stories, we see Jesus showing compassion to people who are suffering and most likely homeless. Their dysfunction dictates their lifestyles. They wear their pain and can't get away from it. These are real stories from the Bible and they remind me of real stories from my own experiences serving the homeless.

Blessed Are the Needy (Matthew 5:1–11)

In the Sermon on the Mount, Jesus refers to people who are lost, hopeless, hungry, and mourning. Sound familiar?

The crowd that has been pursuing Jesus includes those "who were ill with various diseases, those suffering severe pain, the demon-possessed, those having seizures, and the paralyzed" (Matt. 4:24). In our state of helplessness, when we see a crowd of needy people gathering, we often run to hide. Maybe we pace around wringing our hands asking, "What are we going to do?" But Jesus sees them and he sits down. His work is just beginning.

He begins to teach them. He uses words to describe the crowd that sound a lot like the terms we use to describe our homeless friends. He calls them "poor in spirit" (5:3). This I understand. I know what it is to have my spiritual tank on empty—hopeless, having reached the bottom of despair, with nowhere to look but up. And because they are utterly helpless, "they mourn" (v. 4). I meet so many homeless friends who are in a constant state of mourning. They weep for families and for a lifestyle that were lost. Like a tattered and worn-down house on an abandoned highway, their glory years will never be recovered.

"Blessed are the meek" (v. 5) sounds awkward. How can those who are "meek," or humbled, also be blessed? Jesus's audience knew the pious teachings of the Pharisees. He told them that entrance into God's kingdom does not come through the "holier than thou" life of the Law, but through the humble example given by Christ.

Being homeless is humiliating. Many of my homeless friends dig in dumpsters for something to eat, create makeshift toilets behind office buildings, and can't find access to clean clothes or a hot shower. People point, laugh, take photos, or avoid making eye contact and turn to walk in a different direction. If being humiliated was a highway to salvation, there would be a fast lane for the homeless.

However, being meek for the sake of the Lord is different. Believers are called to become less so that Christ can become more (John 3:30). Being forced into humiliation because of socioeconomics, mental health, criminal background, addictions, or situations out of your control almost guarantees humiliation. Yet while humility and meekness sound like close neighbors, in reality they are a world apart.

All of my homeless friends know what it's like to be hungry (and humbled). When they walk into our café, their first question is usually "When is lunch"? But in the Sermon on the Mount Jesus discusses a different form of hunger. He mentions a "hunger and thirst for righteousness." I can't help but think of the words of the prophet Amos:

"The days are coming," declares the Sovereign LORD, "when I will send a famine through the land—not a famine of food or a thirst for water, but a famine of hearing the words of the LORD.'" (Amos 8:11)

I see homeless people searching throughout the city, going from here to there looking for something. To the untrained eye they look like they are wandering aimlessly, but those who care to ask and listen, learn that their search is constant. They are looking for a place to sleep, a source for clean water, a blanket, and a hot meal. But are they looking for something more?

At OurCalling, we focus on spiritual needs—those that are the most necessary, yet the most difficult to find. For those that do hunger and thirst for righteousness, where do they go? Most churches don't allow entrance to anyone with a long beard, a backpack, and the odor of the streets. There are a number of shelters that meet spiritual needs, but almost 80 percent of the homeless in Dallas are not in shelters. And even those who want to go inside may be denied without the right ID, or because of their criminal background. Where are they to go? That is where we come in. We are a discipleship ministry for the homeless.

Jesus continues by speaking of blessings on the merciful, on those who are pure in heart, and on peacemakers (vv. 7–9). When we begin to understand how merciful the Lord has been to us, we can't help but show mercy to others. This is my favorite part of ministry. We rejoice when we see someone transition from being on the receiving line to being on the serving side. When a homeless friend begins showing mercy, the sky opens and they begin to see the light of God's grace in their own life. This isn't a truth limited to the homeless; it is true of all believers when the transformation of the gospel begins to set in.

"Pure in heart" (v. 8) is not a statement of sinlessness, but a recognition of the saving power of Jesus Christ. When we seek and receive His forgiveness, we are freed by the truth (John 8:32) and we receive a purity like no other. I do not think I could count how many lives we have seen changed by this truth. Those with criminal records are often haunted by the crimes of their past. They live in guilt and shame; their past sin holds them in bondage. They suffer endless mental torture. Not only are they disqualified from work, but they are abandoned by family and the church. They wear a scarlet letter that burns with every memory of the past. But when Christ sets them free, they find new life that pours down like rain in the desert.

Peace (v. 9) is rare on the streets. In Dallas, it is illegal to sleep in any public space. No matter where you try to lay your head, someone will harass you. The police will wake you to write you a ticket or move you along. Or someone else will wake you with worse intentions. I remember meeting a new friend who had just been released by the hospital. There were now forty staples in his head and more than seventy stitches. What was the crime that led to this? While he was sleeping in a wooded area, someone decided that they wanted his shoes. They beat my friend in the head with a large piece of concrete. He was awoken two days later by ants dining on the carnage of his face. Peace is rare on the streets.

I have seen young men angry at the world, fresh out of a short prison stint, take their rage out on a homeless senior citizen for sleeping under "their" bridge. Women on the streets face a worse kind of savagery. A victim of domestic violence will come to our office fleeing from brutal torment.

As she is wiping away tears and we are connecting her to law enforcement, medical services, and domestic violence centers, we pause to pray with her. I can hear our staff pray that she would know the peace of God, but too often she stops us and asks what this "peace" is. It seems easier to find a diamond on the streets than a moment of peace.

We have women in our discipleship program who have grown in their relationships with Christ and use their pasts to help others. They may be the most qualified to minister as peacemakers for other women. These disciples may be the first to recognize another woman in need and often stand in the front line to help separate a woman from her aggressor. She is a peacemaker, but that role places her in danger, too.

Sometimes the biggest hell-raisers become the most effective peacemakers. We have a man in our ministry who used to manufacture methamphetamine, cracked safes for a living, and broke more laws than he was ever prosecuted for. But when the love of Christ came into his life, he laid that life behind him. He became a servant of the Most High God. He transitioned from one who caused great suffering to one who helps those who suffer. He transitioned from being a disciple to being a disciple maker, from a Bible study attendee to one who leads and teaches about God's love. He loves to share his testimony of how God's mighty hand has led him to a new role as a peacemaker.

For those whose lives change while they are still on the streets, their lives will not be easy. They will continue to wake up to a world of chaos, watching their friends live in destruction, listening to the cries of those being hunted by the enemy. If they defend the weak, serve the Lord, and represent Christ to this perverse and crooked generation, they will be "persecuted because of righteousness" (v. 10). Yet Jesus assures them, "Blessed are you when people insult you, persecute you and falsely say all kinds of evil against you because of me" (v. 11).

In the Gospel of Mathew, Jesus brings hope to people in desperate need. Those people remind me of many of my homeless friends who struggle and suffer daily. Their survival gives an opportunity for the grace of God to open their eyes to the life-giving truth found in Jesus.

Understanding the "Abnormal" (Mark 5:1–20)

In the fifth chapter of Mark, we read about a different kind of suffering. As Jesus arrives with His disciples on the east side of the Sea of Galilee, an abnormal man comes to greet Him.

What is "normal"? We use this term to define people, places, and things, but do we really have any gauge to measure normal other than our culture or experience? If not, anything outside our experience would thus be abnormal. If a devout Hindu came to my house for dinner as I finished grilling steaks to my "normal" recipe of medium rare, how would my guest evaluate his meal? Having a religion based on reincarnation and valuing the cow as sacred, would he not consider my table filled with steak as abnormal and even revolting? If we really consider our definition of the word and its place in our vernacular, we may be reminded that the Bible sets no standard for normal. In fact, the word is only printed in one place in our home: as a setting on our washing machine. When we say "normal," and when I use it here, it refers to a cultural norm that we are nurtured into believing.

> They went across the lake to the region of the Gerasenes. When Jesus got out of the boat, a man with an impure spirit came from the tombs to meet him. This man lived in the tombs, and no one could bind him anymore, not even with a chain. For he had often been chained hand and foot, but he tore the chains apart and broke the irons on his feet. No one was strong enough to subdue him. Night and day among the tombs and in the hills he would cry out and cut himself with stones. (Mark 5:1–5)

This man lives in a cemetery; he screams all day and night; he cuts himself with stones and runs around naked. I'll just say it: That is weird.

I meet many people like this. When I first started this ministry, my office was a van equipped with Wi-Fi, a wireless printer, and a laptop. I would drive to abnormal places and find scores of people in desperate need of help. I have known people who live in cemeteries, golf courses, abandoned buildings, elevators, cars, wooded encampments, or even underground. Some of them also, like the man in Mark 5, do abnormal things and hurt themselves. Some use criminal activities to support their addictions like prostitution or selling drugs, or scavenge like an urban version of *Survivorman*.

The man in Mark 5 cut himself with stones. I cannot remember the first time I cut myself. I believe I was already in the throes of my addiction that began with pornography. I was not a "frequent cutter"; I only have a few self-inflicted scars. But scar tissue covers the arms and legs of some of my friends in the homeless community. Psychologists use fancy terminology to explain why someone would do this. As a scarred person who serves many with self-inflicted wounds, I fully understand why this happens.

Deep emotional pain is difficult to understand and even harder to control.

Cutting oneself causes pain that is easier to grasp, explain, and control. Self-inflicted physical pain drowns out the internal pain that is more difficult to handle. It sounds crazy, but we all do this to some extent. When I stub my toe, I may slap the wall and wince in pain. One pain replaces another in a sin-cursed world.

But why would someone who perpetrates this crime against themselves be called a "victim"? As with the man in Mark 5, an enemy lies behind this behavior. I believe that the emotional dysfunction at the root of our national epidemic of mental health problems is led by the devil himself. Demons possessed the man in Mark 5, and I believe that the minions of Satan are wreaking havoc in the spiritual battlefield of the mind. I am not associating homelessness or mental illness with demon possession, and I don't think possession is normative. However, after spending thirty years with homeless and mentally ill people, I believe demon possession and oppression are real and too often ignored.

At OurCalling we often draw a crowd that some would call weird or abnormal. I have often overheard our staff say things that would sound quite out of place apart from the context of our ministry. "Put your pants back on." "Please ask your imaginary friend to argue with you more quietly." Or "No, you cannot invite the pigeons in for lunch." We have homeless friends who live in abnormal places, do abnormal things, and hurt themselves.

This disease needs professional help that is often difficult to find. The state of Texas ranks 49th in the country in the amount spent on mental health.[2] And most Christians don't recognize the mental suffering and pain around us. We get our flu shots, wear sunscreen, and send our cancer patients to chemo, but tell someone suffering with a mental illness to "get over it." Similar to other ailments that take us to the doctor, individuals suffering with mental illness need professional medical diagnosis and treatment. When I was diagnosed with malignant melanoma, did I pray and ask others to pray for me? Yes, of course. But I also sought medical treatment from professionals. I will continue to pray and continue to seek professional treatment as long as necessary.

We often don't know what to do with difficult people like the man in Mark 5. We look past their suffering and focus on how their situation makes us feel. Many families of my homeless friends have given up. They have tried everything and yet are left trying to diagnose and treat their loved ones

---

2 http://www.dallasnews.com/news/community-news/dallas/headlines/20130103
-local-mental-health-advocates-seek-parity-in-state-funding-for-programs.ece.

themselves. The dysfunction in someone's life births new dysfunction in the lives of others. Emotional and financial stresses are stacked upon the grief of watching a loved one in pain. At our wit's end, we are open to try anything. Stories of patient abuse, experimental medical procedures, and drug cocktails with fatal results stain our country's history. See how the Gerasenes tried to deal with the possessed man:

> No one could bind him anymore, not even with a chain. For he had often been chained hand and foot, but he tore the chains apart and broke the irons on his feet. No one was strong enough to subdue him. (Mark 5:3-4)

People in my city try a variety of different strategies to "deal" with the homeless and mentally ill. Many organizations work diligently to help. Others don't care; they just want the problem people to go away. If they could, they would lock up these people and their problems and throw away the keys. When a Christian organization like ours shows up to help, they scoff, mock, and try to run us off. Years ago, Dallas police officers would scold me for going under bridges. But today, homeless friends are brought to our doors by officers from the same police force who have seen the success of the gospel within the homeless community. Even secular officers ask us for advice or bring people to us for help. The gospel reminds me that the homeless aren't problems to be solved; they are people to be redeemed.

What the demon-possessed man really needed was not in a pill, straitjacket, or treatment center. He needed Jesus. And when he saw Jesus, his response beautifully acknowledged Jesus as deity.

> When he saw Jesus from a distance, he ran and fell on his knees in front of him. He shouted at the top of his voice, "What do you want with me, Jesus, Son of the Most High God? In God's name don't torture me." (Mark 5:6-7)

The demons speaking through the man recognized something that we often forget about healing: the process is not always pleasant. Other stories of demon possessions in Scripture speak of violent shaking, vomiting, cursing, and screaming. In my experience, this is similar to the detox process of an addict.

Treatment facilities help ease this process with medication, but on the streets, detox from heroin, methamphetamine, and alcohol can produce violent results in those without professional care. Sometimes our Search & Rescue teams see this as they trek throughout Dallas County searching for homeless friends. A hard-core addict who has been without a drug of choice for an extended period of time will be in a terrible medical state. They shake, vomit, curse, and scream. And who tempts them to return to their drug and ease their temporary pain? The enemy and his demons. As believers it is our responsibility to care for, pray for, and lead our new friend to the help they desperately need. They need professional care, but they also need Jesus. I can't count the numerous times we have held someone, waiting for an ambulance, praying that God would heal them.

The man in Mark 5 changed abruptly. Jesus sent the demons into pigs, but the real transformation occurred in the man. The people from the town gathered around in amazement.

> When they came to Jesus, they saw the man who had been possessed by the legion of demons, sitting there, dressed and in his right mind; and they were afraid. (Mark 5:15)

Take note of what they saw. The abnormal man who had been in an abnormal place doing abnormal things—was different. He had been running and screaming in a cemetery day and night, naked and cutting himself. And here he is a moment later, perfectly normal. Dressed (a striking improvement) and in his right mind. How did this happen? Had they not tried everything in their power and failed? Jesus has finally done what they wanted—and how do they respond? With fear.

Jesus has just done what they couldn't do for this man, no matter how hard they had tried. But instead of thanking Jesus or pleading with Him to heal other people, they are afraid. Before we judge them too harshly, let's remember that people commonly responded to Jesus this way when He revealed His glory. Just before the disciples encountered the demon-possessed man, they had been in a boat thrashed by a storm. Panicked, they awoke Jesus, who calmed the storm with His voice. Their response, too, was fear (Mark 4:40–41). Yet Jesus' fearful power should encourage us that He can do amazing things in seemingly impossible situations.

As the story continues in Mark, Jesus agrees to leave as the people had asked Him.

> As Jesus was getting into the boat, the man who had been demon-possessed begged to go with him. Jesus did not let him, but said, "Go home to your own people and tell them how much the Lord has done for you, and how he has had mercy on you." (Mark 5:18–19)

OurCalling serves thousands of individuals, each of whom represents a broken, suffering family and whose dysfunction reflects the curse and generational sin. When God heals the individual—and He often does—the individual in turn must reach that broken home. Somewhere today, a family needs to see and hear what the Lord has done. They need to know how Jesus has shown mercy.

Parents and children frequently call me looking for their loved ones. We love setting up family reunions and interventions. Many times, though, the calls come too late. Often, I only meet the suffering family of a homeless friend when I perform my friend's funeral. The family never knew the person I know. They only saw brokenness, a selfish prodigal who left and destroyed a family in the process. They never knew that their loved one suffered from a serious mental illness. One woman had abandoned her five children. They assumed she loved the world more than them, that maybe an addiction was leading her away from responsibility. They never knew how sick their mother was, or that she was trying to protect them. Before the children's father was imprisoned, he had targeted her with violence. She believed that if he was released from jail, he would return to hurt her and the children. Her mental illness fueled this belief and made her shelter-resistant. On the streets, though, she was an evangelist. She carried Bibles in English and Spanish; she shared Scripture and Bible stories with women throughout Dallas. At her funeral, I had the privilege of sharing the story of the mom the children had never known.

Committed to Help (Luke 5:17–26)

We hear about another suffering individual in Luke: a paralytic. I know many homeless individuals suffering with paralysis, with missing limbs, birth defects, terminal illness, and various other forms of disability. I have found many in deplorable conditions.

Many of these individuals qualify for a relatively new initiative called "housing first." In a race to get people off of the street, cities across the country are housing the homeless at an alarming rate. This sounds like a great idea—provide safe housing combined with support services.

Actually, most homeless shelters are built on this model. They provide semi-permanent housing and support services designed to help the person develop long-term goals and skills to maintain themselves for long-term success. These programs transition the person into long-term housing where they will eventually live a sustainable lifestyle.

However, "housing first" initiatives usually skip the shelters and the rehabilitation process altogether. They take a dysfunctional person off the street and immediately place them into housing. It's relatively cheap to pay for someone's rent, which makes an easy "win" if the goal is relocation. But to help a dysfunctional person learn a new way to live, the financial burden extends far beyond rent and utilities.

In our city, housing options may come quickly, but supportive programs are lacking. Recently I met with the director of a veterans program who told me they could get someone qualified within 48 hours. When I asked about support services, I was told that a case worker would visit every other week. How do we expect someone to learn a sustainable lifestyle without sufficient support?

One couple abandoned by "housing first" stands out in my mind. They received their new apartment through a lightning-speed program. These programs, so focused on speed, do not take time to evaluate the real reasons why someone is homeless or how to help them not repeat the same process. This couple suffered severe mental health and developmental issues. The wife was schizophrenic and bipolar, while the husband had learning and physical disabilities.

They found our hotline number while digging through a dumpster for a meal. When I visited them, I found that even with a new apartment, they were still functionally homeless. They had never lived on their own, didn't know how to cook or provide for themselves. They were living in absolute filth. I came to their apartment in the middle of a sweltering Texas summer and expected to find cool relief inside. But they didn't know how to work the thermostat; they even had the heater on. They were starving, filthy, and dehydrated. They had no furniture, toilet paper, plates, cups, or blankets. They lived in a pile of trash in the living room, scavenging in the neighborhood dumpsters for anything they could find to help them survive.

When I asked where they got food, the husband told me he would walk through the apartment complex at night and take any pet food he found sitting outside. Remnants on the floor confirmed that they were surviving on the neighbor's cat food.

This couple was in their late 70s. Their newfound "solution" to their homelessness had only added insult and more suffering to a lifetime of struggle. When I met them, they had been in their new apartment for more than four months; no one had visited them. Where were the supportive services they needed? Why were they placed here without any visits or follow-through? Where does the assistance of the government end and the responsibility of the church begin?

In Luke 5, a group of committed friends brought a paralyzed man to Jesus for healing. Jesus had become so popular, though, that the mass of people lined up to see Him kept these friends from reaching the door of the house. The men were undeterred. They knew Jesus could heal their friend; they were determined to bring their friend to Him. As believers, we need this type of resolve when we see people suffering. Are we willing to go to any length to bring people to Jesus?

> When they could not find a way to do this because of the crowd, they went up on the roof and lowered him on his mat through the tiles into the middle of the crowd, right in front of Jesus. When Jesus saw their faith, he said, "Friend, your sins are forgiven." (Luke 5:19–20)

Since they couldn't get through the door, they decided to go through the roof. What a shock the houseguests must have had! On a day almost two thousand years before electric lights, light suddenly began to shine in the ceiling of the house as the roof was opened. I imagine a scene from *Mission Impossible*—a man hanging like a human piñata in front of the crowd. Jesus sees this and speaks: "Friend, your sins are forgiven" (v. 20).

There are a few things in this story that I find amazing. The first is the faith of the man's friends. Today, we will rarely cross the street to help someone. But these men walked past the crowd, found a way onto the roof, dug a hole through the ceiling, and lowered their friend in. They risked public ridicule, rebuke from Jesus, and even their own safety. I can't imagine first-century roofs were built to structurally withstand a man-sized hole! They did whatever it took to bring their friend to Jesus.

Today, if we knew Jesus was across town, would we be so committed to our suffering friends? Would we risk the crowd, the awkwardness of the situation, and public ridicule? Or would we chicken out and only click "like" on Facebook when we saw a picture of someone else doing it?

Jesus is not across town today. He's sitting at the right hand of the Father. We can't take people across town to see Jesus. Instead, we can do more. Since we are made holy, filled with the Spirit, and ambassadors of the Lord Himself, we can take what God has given us to suffering people. We can't bring sick people to Jesus, but we can bring Jesus to them.

Notice that Luke says Jesus responded "when [He] saw their faith" (5:20). The friends' faith prompted the Lord to respond. Maybe God hasn't moved in a suffering person's life because He's waiting on you to move first. Now, I don't think faith is a requirement for healing; many people were healed in the New Testament who had no prior faith in Jesus. But in this particular instance, Jesus was moved by the faith shown by the people committed to helping the suffering man. And He responds perfectly and beautifully.

He tells the man, "Friend, your sins are forgiven." The man was brought to Jesus because he was paralyzed. He couldn't walk; he spent his days lying on a mat. He depended on others for survival. He couldn't even get up to see Jesus. Jesus' first reaction, though, was not to offer a diagnosis or a cure. In fact, Jesus didn't even mention the man's crippling condition. Why?

When you take a loved one to the hospital, you expect people in the emergency room to be absolute professionals. You don't want them to be distracted by minor problems when major problems are more urgent. Wouldn't you be upset if you took your child who could barely breathe to a doctor, only to have the doctor focus on a splinter?

Jesus momentarily set aside the man's minor paralysis because He saw a major issue: sin. Jesus diagnosed the biggest problem and offered a permanent cure.

Jesus looked past the crowd and the chaos of a man hanging from the ceiling and saw the problem of the heart. Do we do this? When we see a homeless man who reeks of cheap liquor and urine, do we recognize the heart problem? Or are we distracted by the smell? Do we wonder how he could walk around looking like that, or do we embrace him and bring Jesus to his greatest need? Are we committed to curing the major issues, or are we too squeamish about the minor things? Maybe that stinky homeless man doesn't care for his hygiene because he believes no one cares for him. Maybe he can't forgive himself for the sins that he has committed, therefore he believes he is making penance for his past. Jesus offers the only eternal solution for this man's biggest problem. He offers forgiveness.

I have a homeless friend who lives this problem today. He refuses to go to shelters, resists treatment or help, and uses meth and alcohol to dull the pain of his past. Once, while he was dealing heroin in New York, he knowingly sold some bad drugs that ended up killing four people. Because he doesn't understand the forgiveness offered by Christ, today he looks for fights and lets himself get beaten to bear penance for the past mistakes. He was recently released from the hospital with eyes swollen shut and staples in his head; he had been beaten with a bicycle wheel. I told him about Jesus and the forgiveness that He offers. I told him that God offers a new life through the blood of Jesus that cleanses sins. Today, he still believes that only by spilling more of his own blood will he find forgiveness. Please pray for my suffering friend.

Meeting Real Needs (John 5:1–9)

The Gospel of John also shows Jesus serving and healing many people who resemble my suffering homeless friends. In the fifth chapter, Jesus returns to Jerusalem for one of the Jewish festivals.

> Some time later, Jesus went up to Jerusalem for one of the Jewish festivals. Now there is in Jerusalem near the Sheep Gate a pool, which in Aramaic is called Bethesda and which is surrounded by five covered colonnades. Here a great number of disabled people used to lie—the blind, the lame, the paralyzed. (John 5:1–3)

Suffering people often congregate around some thing or service that they believe will meet a need, whether the need is real or felt. For example, people gather in hospitals, rehab centers, homeless shelters, and even churches because of real needs. But people also congregate around sources that meet felt needs—these seem necessary, but may actually cause other problems or highlight more urgent needs. For example, the local bar meets felt needs, but may also highlight the real need for addiction recovery. Other places where people gather to satisfy felt needs might include liquor stores, casinos, favorite panhandling spots, or even people or places that promise faith healing. These groups gather because they feel like needs are being met, but their gathering reveals real needs that remain unfulfilled.

Encampments under bridges exemplify this problem. Some of my homeless friends go to these places because they refuse to submit to the rules and structure of a shelter or other established environment. However, as soon as more than one person camps under the same bridge, they begin making their own camp "rules" and enforcing them on anyone who wants to stay there. The rules are arbitrary and subject to change at any time, just like the rules they hate from a shelter. They may not like community at the shelters, but they long to form relationships and build their own community. Even though they complain about the homeless people who stay in shelters, they continue to build their encampment with those same types of people. The very problems they would meet in a shelter arise in the encampment, so they leave to start a new one. The cycle repeats.

Many homeless friends also gather around faith healing and "get-healed-quick" solutions. I personally believe God has a market on the healing business, so when I see someone claiming to heal people, it gives me the creeps. I hope they can and wish they could, yet I haven't found anyone willing to let me take them to the local hospital to empty the building. Think of the scene if we could walk from ward to ward, healing everyone in every bed, in every wheelchair, and on every surgery table!

Yet people still come downtown to host faith-healing services. My homeless friends flock to these, get their hopes up, have an amazing healing experience. The next day brings a horrible hangover when they realize that their right leg is still two inches shorter than their left. One homeless woman was awarded more than $20,000 through a government settlement. Instead of securing housing, she gave it to a faith healer so she, too, could be healed. Today she is still sick and homeless. The enemy preys on those who are suffering and oppresses them with false hope.

The pool of Bethesda was a place where a "great number of disabled people used to lie—the blind, the lame, the paralyzed" (John 5:3). Why would they come there? Was a real need being met, or was it only a felt need? Was there real healing in the water, or just false hope?

I believe that it was a cruel joke. Imagine disabled people racing to the water—what if the paralyzed man had actually made it in? How would he get out? I can't find any evidence that any real healing ever took place. I also can't find evidence of any special healing spot recorded elsewhere in the Bible. Do suffering people believe that they can go to "one place" and see "one person" who can actually heal them? Ever since the Fall, suffering people have been fed lies to give them false hope. The snake made Eve believe she was suffering because she couldn't eat from one single tree in the Garden. She believed in false hope that she would be "like God" if she would only follow the snake's instructions. This false hope led her to disobey God; the curse of sin came as the result of her and Adam. Even in this story in Luke, had the man known who was in Jerusalem, he wouldn't have been waiting and watching for bubbling water in a pool; he would have been seeking the living water—Jesus Christ.

I have another theory as to why the disabled were gathered at this particular location. The pool stood near the Sheep Gate, where people would bring in sacrificial animals to sell to pilgrims who could not bring their own. I don't know any first-century disabled people, but I do know that twenty-first-century homeless people often gather near places where they can make a buck. Many take advantage of disabilities to panhandle for cash. Even those without a disability will grab a pair of crutches, wheelchair, or leg brace in order to guilt passers-by into a donation. Money would have passed through the Sheep Gate on a regular basis; it would have been an ideal location for panhandling.

I am adamant that you should *never* give money to a panhandler. I believe that cash gifts to the poor (in developed countries, at least) only hurt people. While the Bible instructs us to care for the poor, it never specifies that we give them cash. The disciples in the early church recruited deacons for the purpose of distributing food, not money, to the poor (Acts 6:1–6). Jesus Himself said:

> For I was hungry and you gave me something to eat, I was thirsty and
> you gave me something to drink, I was a stranger and you invited me in,
> I needed clothes and you clothed me, I was sick and you looked after me,
> I was in prison and you came to visit me. (Matt. 25:35–36)

Notice that He never said "You rolled down your window and gave me $2 to ignore my real need and appease your conscience." Scripture instructs us to meet real needs.

When you give money to homeless people, you are killing my friends. In reality, you are paying for their drugs and sex. God has entrusted your money to you as a sacred stewardship. He gave you that money to use for His glory. When that money leaves your pocket and ends up hurting someone, you are responsible. Arguing "I prayed over the money" while handing it to a dope-fiend is as ignorant as praying over a donation to a known terrorist organization. God expects us to be more responsible with His gifts. Numerous times I have lain on the ground holding a homeless friend, waiting for an ambulance—as a result of panhandling for cash. I can't count the number of women I have seen abused because of cash. Either she was assaulted because she didn't earn enough in panhandling, or some guy panhandled enough to buy her for his own pleasure and he assaulted her. Either way, that's not the return of God's investment that we should seek.

Some may scoff at my theory of the correlation of the crowd of disabled people and the Sheep Gate. Still, I have seen many homeless people take advantage of physical disabilities to scam money from well-meaning people, churches, and our government. There are many people with real needs who need multiple forms of assistance and I am so proud to live in a society where help is available. I think these needs should be met in ways that provide accountability. Let us not forget: assistance without accountability can bring an avalanche.

Back in John's story, Jesus asks the disabled man an awkward question: "Do you want to get well?" (John 5:6). At first, the question sounds crazy. This man had been sitting by the healing pool for years and Jesus asks him if he wants to get well? Yet I have asked that question time and time again. I don't have the power to heal like Jesus did, but I ask the same question and get very different responses.

At OurCalling, we probably host between one hundred fifty and two hundred fifty homeless friends each day. If you were to take the time to get to know a few of our friends, you might end up asking them the same question. Some suffering people are actually comfortable in their pain. They have grown used to it and developed elaborate coping mechanisms.

Drugs are one such mechanism. I have never met anyone who really likes heroin, meth, crack, or alcohol. Addicts usually hate themselves and hate their reality, so they find escape from reality in their drug of choice. The chase of the next high is the pursuit of relief from suffering.

I have asked so many homeless friends, "Do you want to get well?" or maybe, "Do you want to stop your addiction?" Fear of change and history of failure often paralyze the thought of "one more try." My friends in their sixties have been using hard-core drugs for so long they can't remember a time of sobriety. They are terrified of their future and paralyzed by their past. I tell them they are too old to be playing these silly games; it's time to make a real change.

I have taken hundreds of people to rehab. Most of those trips were a waste of gas and time. I was young; I naively assumed that anyone who was willing to take a car ride was ready for the change required in rehab. Most of those trips left me with an emotional high because "I had helped them." A few days later, I would be hit with an emotional hangover when I found them back in the same place, doing the same destructive habits. Most people I took to rehab only wanted to please me or to get a free night's stay with air conditioning, good food, and a clean bed. Now our staff has developed a rubric for rehab that we use to determine someone's ability and desire to change. We do not want to waste time with someone who isn't ready if there is another who is.

After years of ministry, I have found the secret to changing someone who has been stuck in the same cycle for years. It's not fast and it's not easy. It takes the most time and requires the greatest investment. The secret is *trust.*

If we think about the biggest questions in life, we are all left with doubt and therefore need to trust someone. Whom will you marry? Where will you live? What will your career be for the rest of your life? Hurry, choose now! We have to think deeply about those questions and others that may have lasting implications. We need to surround ourselves with people we can trust. We may ask our parents, our friends, even our grandparents or life-long family friends. We would never ask a stranger whom we should marry, or what career path to take. So why would a stranger trust us with major change? If you know a suffering person who needs to make a major change, you may not be able to help them until they can trust you. Only after you have built an intimate layer of trust will they consider any major change you are suggesting.

When Jesus asked the man, "Do you want to be healed?," the man didn't know or trust Jesus. He immediately explained that he couldn't win the race to get into the magical water to be healed. This is ludicrous. I can imagine the disciples nearby rolling their eyes at the man. He is sitting with Jesus, the Healer. He is in the presence of the One about whom John earlier wrote "through him all things were made; without him nothing was made that has been made" (John 1:3). The paralyzed man does not know to whom he is talking. He has no knowledge of who Jesus is and no faith in the Son of Man.

> Then Jesus said to him, "Get up! Pick up your mat and walk." At once the man was cured; he picked up his mat and walked. (John 5:8–9)

I wish I could do that. I have prayed for healing for countless people and I have seen God do some amazing things, but I can't heal anyone myself. If I could, I would make a tour of every homeless camp that our teams visit. Then I would visit every hospital, homeless shelter, and rehab facility. Then I might visit a few government offices, because we all know they need some healing. But I can't heal. I've asked for that gift, but I don't think it's in God's plan. What is in God's plan is for me to introduce suffering people to the Healer, to tell them about Jesus and ask them if they want to be healed.

Introducing Jesus

During His time on earth, Jesus met suffering people with great needs that only He could meet. People in our own cities look the same. A homeless man may have the same needs as you, yet he doesn't have the creative means of hiding his pain or the societal structure that you and I rely on. He looks on the outside the way he feels on the inside. However, his greatest need is not a blanket and a bottle of water. He needs Jesus. It is our privilege and command to introduce the man on the street to the King of Glory.

Discussion Questions

1. What needs described in the Sermon of the Mount are common in everyone?
2. How does our definition of "normal" affect our opinion of others? How does this affect our ideas and strategy about ministry?
3. To what extent should we go to bring Jesus to sick people? What are the barriers in doing so?
4. How can we better communicate the true hope and healing of Christ to those in need?

Resources for Further Study

Books

Steve Corbett and Brian Fikkert, *When Helping Hurts: How to Alleviate Poverty without Hurting the Poor* (Chicago: Moody Press, 2014).

Jimmy Dorrell, *Trolls and Truth: 14 Realities about Today's Church That We Don't Want to See* (Birmingham: New Hope, 2006).

Mike Yankoski, *Under the Overpass: A Journey of Faith on the Streets of America*, rev. ed. (Colorado Springs, CO: Multnomah, 2005).

EIGHT

Redeeming a Life after Suicide:
The New Normal

BILL BRYAN

> Be anxious for nothing, but in everything by prayer and suppli-
> cation with thanksgiving let your requests be made known to
> God. And the peace of God, which surpasses all comprehen-
> sion, will guard your hearts and your minds in Christ Jesus. Fi-
> nally, brethren, whatever is true, whatever is honorable, what-
> ever is right, whatever is pure, whatever is lovely, whatever is of
> good repute, if there is any excellence and if anything worthy of
> praise, dwell on these things. The things you have learned and
> received and heard and seen in me, practice these things, and
> the God of peace will be with you. (Phil. 4:6–9.)[1]

It was just a normal afternoon in Springfield, Missouri. The sun was shin-
ing, and people were window-shopping and strolling the streets with
loved ones. But on the sixth floor of the downtown medical arts building,
a psychiatrist was meeting with a family—a father and a mother and their
little boy, Bill. After meeting with the father, the doctor spoke to the mother
alone as the little boy and his father sat just outside. The office door stood
slightly ajar; bits of conversation trickled out. The doctor explained to the
mother that there was no cure for the kind of depression her husband was
struggling with and recommended that she commit him to an insane asylum.
The doctor came out and asked the family to wait while he consulted with

---

1 All Scripture quotations are from the NASB. All emphases are mine.

some of his colleagues about some specific recommendations. While he was gone, the three walked into the lobby. The sad father picked up his little boy, kissed him, and said, "I love you, son." Then he put down his child and ran as hard as he could toward the end of the hall. Propelled forward as if being chased, he crashed through the nearest window and dove headfirst to his death six floors below.

I was that little boy, and that was the last sight I had of my father, Devereaux Bryan.

My mother, Elaine, would have followed my father to her own death out of impulse, but a nurse standing close by tackled her legs. They said my mother's screams could be heard all over downtown Springfield. Minutes later a neighbor found me wandering alone on the first floor of the medical building. The trauma of that moment—my mother's screams, the shattered window glass—has forever colored my view of the world.

Following my father's suicide, my mother and I moved in with her parents and my teenaged aunt. My mother suffered an emotional breakdown and was effectively unable to care for me for the next two years. My aunt became my babysitter; my grandparents became my surrogate parents. In the sense that I had quickly landed in a place of some basic security, things were relatively good for me. I forged a deep, life-long bond with these members of my family. However, it was often unclear exactly who was in charge of things around our new home. Most of the time my grandparents and my aunt raised me. However, my mom would come out of her stupor from time to time and briefly assert herself as my parent—usually in the form of discipline. A few years after my father's death, my mother remarried and a stepfather was added to the mix. Throughout the next decade I moved through various locations and permutations of family. My life became increasingly filled with confusion and anxiety.

To be perfectly honest, I think both my mother and I subconsciously wished to be free of each other. It wasn't that we didn't care for each other—I loved my mother and she loved me—but we constantly reminded each other of the tragedy that had gutted our family. I would have preferred to go on living with my grandparents rather than with my mother and stepfather. I suspect my mother felt the same, but she saw such a decision as an admission of failure as a parent. So we muddled along in our dysfunctional home, and our resentment toward each other reached a fever pitch. Although I had put my faith in Jesus Christ as a child, I wasn't really walking with Christ as an adolescent. I became especially surly and bitter in my relationship to my mother and stepfather. Suffice it to say that home life in my teenage years was a storm.

My mother, my stepfather, and I moved to Wichita, Kansas, where the storm continued. At her wit's end with my behavior, my mother called the local pastor's wife for help in dealing with her rebellious son—me! The pastor's wife agreed to have her daughter invite me to church, and although I had no interest in church, the pastor's daughter, Shirley, enchanted me. We became fast friends, and she soon had a positive effect on me. As I turned from my attitude of rebellion, I realized that Shirley possessed all the qualities I could ever dream of in a spouse. I knew beyond a shadow of a doubt that I had to be with this woman. Upon graduating from high school we both entered Wheaton College, and it was there that God continued to assert His grip on my life. My studies of the Bible and my activities at school all pointed toward a life in vocational ministry. As I completed my college degree, I began making plans to attend Dallas Theological Seminary (DTS) in order to be trained as a pastor.

After I graduated from DTS in 1962, Shirley and I moved to Oklahoma City, where I began working as an assistant pastor at a local church. Things were going well for us. By that time we had added our first two sons to our family, and I had completed another graduate degree, this time in psychology. A local psychologist whom I had gotten to know through my studies asked me to sit on a consortium of ministers dealing with pastoral counseling issues.

Then it happened.

At the first meeting of that group, each member was asked to give a brief overview of his journey leading up to that point. After I told my story, the group asked, "Bill, have you ever gotten closure on your father's death?"

"I'm not sure I know what you mean," I replied.

"What we mean is—have you ever *closed the lid on your dad's casket and shoveled the dirt on his grave* so that you can go on with your life?" Their stark words struck a chord in me. Perhaps they were right. Maybe I needed to deal with my father's suicide once and for all. But what might that entail? I began making plans for a trip to where it all began: Springfield, Missouri.

My first stop was to visit some of my father's family. Katie and Opal, two of my father's sisters (and my aunts), greeted me with overwhelming affection even though they hadn't seen me in more than twenty-five years. They regaled me with stories about my father and told me what a wonderful man he had been. They also told me how proud he would have been of me. Feeling my father's love vicariously through my aunts was a wonderful way to begin my pilgrimage, but I had further to go. I stopped next at Greystone Cemetery, the site of my father's grave. While I stood over the grassy spot, a profound sense of loss—and the anxiety that accompanied it—rushed over me again. I fell to my knees and began to weep over my father's grave. As difficult as this moment was, I knew that I still had one more place to visit.

Although much of downtown Springfield had certainly changed over the past decades, I instantly recognized the building from which my father leapt to his death. I slowly made my way up the many stairs to the sixth floor, retracing the path I had taken as a child when I unwittingly tried to leave this place behind. Yet this time I was no longer a child fleeing a tragedy. As I climbed each stair I was now Abraham carrying the one I loved to an inevitable sacrifice. I reached the sixth floor and looked around. The configuration had changed, but new paint and a few moved walls could not disguise where I was standing: this was where I had last seen my father. This was also my Mount Moriah (Gen. 22:2). In that dizzying moment I spiritually laid my father on the altar and gave him away to God. In that instant I felt I had finally been freed from the anxiety and anguish that had been gnawing at me my entire life.

But as Shirley and I began our drive back to Oklahoma, I felt tinges of that same old struggle seeping into my heart and mind. Had I not just said goodbye to my father in the exact same place he had once said goodbye to me? Would I never be rid of these painful feelings? While understanding the source of my anxiety helped me understand why I was the way I was, it in no way excused me for constantly giving in to worry. As Larry Crabb writes, we know that "the real culprit behind all non-organically caused human distress: a steadfast determination to remain independent of God and still make life work." This entire trip had still not fully rid me of the anguish of my father's death, but I felt I was now at a moment of readiness. Overcome, I pulled the car to the side of the road and began calling out to God. *Why did this have to happen? Why did you take my father from me, God? I don't want to carry this weight any longer. I'm in bondage to anxiety and worry. Please help me, God!* My sweet wife, Shirley, suggested that we search Scripture to see what it had to say about facing my fears with God's help.

As a result of the suicide of my father, I was often besieged with worry. Worry became my greatest spiritual struggle. For the next few years, Shirley and I studied God's Word to see what it had to say that might help me with my worry. The more I learned, the more I tried to put it into practice. In the past I had spent far too much time waiting until life's difficulties had already surrounded me with anxiety before attempting to deal with the situation. Thus my problems would seem to grow exponentially in my mind. I discovered that small worries had a tendency to become large problems when I ignored them. It became obvious that one of the best things I could do was to shift from being *reactive* to *proactive* when it came to addressing my worries. I needed to plan ahead so that anxiety wouldn't get a foothold and create an avalanche of worry and fear. I needed to develop a *planned biblical response* so that when I felt the onset of anxiety, I was prepared to respond.

As I gradually started to fill the vacuum of anxiety with Scripture, I began to see real progress. I certainly wasn't immune to worry, but the struggle slowly grew easier. When faced with a problem (and the ensuing temptation to worry), I would meditate on God's Word and move the difficult issue from the center of my life to a place far removed in my mind. It wasn't that I was trying to repress the emotions or deny that something troubling was going on. In fact, I fully owned whatever problem was before me. However, my goal was to see it moved from a place of focus to a place ruled by God's peace. After years searching the Scriptures, Shirley and I found many Scripture passages that speak to the issue of anxiety, but we settled on Philippians 4:6–9 as the key to defending ourselves from oppressive worry and fear. After considerable meditation and practice, Shirley and I eventually distilled the truths in this passage into a simple formula we like to call Five Ps in a Pod.

1. PRAYER: "Be anxious for nothing, but in everything *by prayer and supplication . . .*" While prayer can be a wonderful time of intimacy with our heavenly Father, I like to think of this particular prayer as an SOS to the Savior. It's a cry for help—*God, it's me. Help, I'm feeling the onset of anxiety.* God isn't at all surprised by what's going on in our lives. He already knows of our problem because He is a God who exists outside of time. While our earthly struggles may come as a shock to us, they certainly don't catch God off guard. When we pray these prayers for help, we're simply getting on the same page as God—He is already there waiting for us to call out to Him. As the old song lyrics say, "Oh, what peace we often forfeit, oh, what needless pain we bear all because we do not carry everything to God in prayer."

2. PRAISE: "*. . . with thanksgiving* let your requests be made known to God . . ." In this phase I picture my life as a big circle. As I sit in the center and look out, I begin by thanking and praising God for the things on the edges of my life. These things may seem far away from my current struggles, but since I am not yet able to praise God for my struggles, I praise Him for what I can. I might begin by thanking Him for my very life. Perhaps I praise Him for His love and salvation. Or for my sons, my daughters-in-law, and my nine precious grandchildren.

I might thank Him for the example of the biblical saints in the "Hall of Faith" in Hebrews 11 and how they endured or overcame their own struggles. And of course, if the saints of old can overcome trials by God's power, then I suppose there's a chance for me, too. Maybe God can add me to the twenty-first-century "Hall of Faith." At this point I'm beginning to move inward in my circle of life. I can see that God is, and always has been, at work in the lives of His children. After praising Him enough, I eventually find that His Spirit has given me the ability to thank Him even for the very struggle I'm facing. After all, it has driven me to God in desperate dependence so that I can echo Paul when he says, "I will rather boast about my weaknesses so that the power of Christ may dwell in me" (2 Cor. 12:9). I finally reach a point of total resignation and admit that I cannot solve this on my own. I need God to act within me.

3. PEACE: ". . . and the *peace* of God, which surpasses all comprehension, will guard your hearts and your minds in Christ Jesus." This is a promise! If we offer prayer with praise, then we are guaranteed that the peace of Christ will guard our hearts and minds. Peace is like a sentinel keeping watch on a city wall who paces back and forth to keep watch and protect the city from predators. God's peace encircles my life and wards off any and all predators such as negative thoughts, anxiety, and fear.

4. POSITIVE THOUGHTS: "Finally, brethren, whatever is true, whatever is honorable, whatever is right, whatever is pure, whatever is lovely, whatever is of good repute, if there is any excellence and if anything worthy of praise, *dwell on these things.*" Fill your life with positive thoughts. I'm not talking about positive *possibilities* or delusional thinking; those are not what Paul is talking about. The positive thoughts I'm talking about relate to the Lord. When I think about Him and the truth He has given us in His Word, it gets easier to shift my concentration away from things that cause anxiety. By far the most positive thought I can entertain centers on the person and work of Jesus Christ—His life, His character, and His ministry. Positive thoughts are not in themselves a cure for life's problems, but a mind that dwells on the things of God will not easily succumb to the anxiety that often accompanies our troubles.

5. PRACTICE: "The things you have learned and received and heard and seen in me, *practice these things,* and the God of peace will be with you." Give it a shot! Try practicing these steps and see if God works

through them. Like most things in life, we will get better at this with repetition. And as we practice the Five Ps, they will become more and more natural to us. This final *P* in the pod is so important because it helps us build the reflex of seeking God's help when we see anxiety and fear coming our way. God desires for us to come to Him, and He already knows how best to care for us in every struggle we will ever face.

To be sure, my newfound peace faced numerous challenges. Not long after my fateful return to Springfield to revisit my father's suicide, Shirley and I suffered the death of our third son at birth. To make the tragedy even worse, I was severely ill with hepatitis at the time, and my precious wife found herself delivering the baby in our bathroom since I didn't even have the strength to get out of bed. As if all that was not enough, the hospital lab lost our son's body. We could not even bury him properly. These were harrowing events to say the least. While the Five Ps in no way negated our loss, they did help to extinguish the flames of grievous worry that erupted at that time. I suppose that God wanted to make sure that I had ample opportunity to utilize that final *P* in the list: PRACTICE! Life never seemed to lack trials and tribulations for long. Whether from a string of car accidents—some causing serious injury—or a child who embarked on a decades-long addiction to drugs and alcohol, anxiety was always waiting to creep into my soul and wreak havoc. I was ever thankful that God had shown us the five principles that could help us face our struggles, no matter how difficult.

Through these biblical principles I have been able to see God's work in diminishing the presence and power of anxiety in my life. But what about someone who struggles with something other than worry? I am convinced that God's Word can provide similar support no matter the struggle. Whether your trial comes in the form of anger, covetousness, pride, or a pattern of lust—for power, approbation, food, sex, etc.—each of these areas are dealt with either by precept or principle in God's Word. The method is straightforward, though not always easy. First, we must go to the Bible and collect everything we can find that deals with our particular issue. Second, we need to synthesize those truths into something manageable—like the Five Ps—that we can access easily when trouble rears its head. Third, we must memorize our new distillation of God's truth for our particular struggle. Finally, we must follow through and live out the principles that God has given to us. With these four steps, it is possible to construct a planned biblical response for any affliction that comes our way.

During these decades of practicing the Five Ps, Shirley and I discovered that we needed more than just a method. The recipe of the Five Ps can easily amount to nothing more than a mantra if we're not careful. This is why God has provided three agents of change in our lives: God's Spirit, God's Word, and God's people.

We know that we are ultimately powerless apart from the Holy Spirit. Unless we submit to the Spirit, there is no chance of success. Similarly, the Bible provides the basis for this very plan of attack against worry. These aren't just good moral principles to make one's life better; these are God's promises from His Word. They are trustworthy and powerful. Finally, God's people embody His love in our lives. We are often tempted to endure difficulty alone and suffer in silence. We might even congratulate ourselves on the fact that we aren't a burden to those around us. However, God often works powerfully in our lives through His children. Although it may confound our logic, God has chosen human beings as His preferred vehicle for getting things done in this world. Therefore we should always be ready for God to use those around us to provide comfort and strength as we face adversity and anxiety. By continually practicing the Five Ps in conjunction with these agents of God's change, I have seen anxiety steadily diminish in my life. I have learned to walk longer distances without falling.

Interestingly enough, Shirley and I have also seen God's hand at work through things that are unique to our lives, most noticeably through music. We are both trained musicians, and we find great joy in both listening to and making music. Over the years it has been astonishing to see how God has visited us through songs, both secular and sacred, that have either soothed our troubled minds or brought perspective to our suffering. A number of years back, as we were going through another round of life's difficulties, we heard Tanya Tucker's song "Two Sparrows in a Hurricane" on the radio. The lyrics captured our hearts and minds.

We latched onto the image of the sparrows, and our minds turned immediately to the words of Matthew 6:26–27: "Look at the birds of the air, that they do not sow, nor reap nor gather into barns, and *yet* your heavenly Father feeds them. Are you not worth much more than they? And who of you by being worried can add a *single* hour to his life?" We thought about how we often feel like those two little birds facing a storm, and the song reminded us to stay nested in God's Word as we wrestle with life's many challenges. It may seem strange to have the lyrics to a country music song direct one's thoughts toward the Lord, but that's just what this song did for Shirley and me. In many ways it has become our theme song since then. There are numerous other times when music has been a source of happiness or relief for us, and it brings great comfort to know that our Savior knows us so intimately—and loves us so perfectly—that He will provide for us through vehicles that are unique to our personalities.

The experiences that I had on my long and arduous journey have certainly helped shape me in my life in ministry. My years as a pastor were challenging and rewarding, yet I had always harbored a deep desire to do something different than pastor a church.

In 1970, Shirley asked me a question that later seemed almost prophetic. "If I could have any job in the world, what would it be?" My answer was very clear—I wanted to be the chaplain at DTS. This was not at all to say that I didn't enjoy my role as a church pastor, but the variety of hats that the chaplain wore—pastor, teacher, mentor, counselor, music leader—sounded compelling to me. However, given that my "dream job" seemed so specific and unlikely, I pressed on in my role as a pastor, which I also loved.

For the next fifteen years I worked as an associate pastor and senior pastor at two churches in two states. And then, in the summer of 1984, I was in Pagosa Springs, Colorado, presenting at a Bible conference alongside Dr. Donald Campbell, then executive vice president of DTS. At lunch one day, Dr. Campbell mentioned to me that the seminary would be looking for a new chaplain since the current one would be stepping down at the end of the year. I responded, "Well, I just might throw my hat in the ring."

"It's already in the ring!" he responded. "We've been considering you as a possibility."

The rest, as they say, is history. But it became obvious to me during my time at DTS that I had been uniquely prepared for this specific position. Because of my pastoral gifts, musical ability, counseling proficiency, and heart for discipleship, I flourished in my role as chaplain. Beyond that, the seminary appointed me as an associate professor of pastoral ministries—a position that led to me directing and teaching the required pastoral counseling course for the Th.M. program. God was making real Paul's words in 2 Corinthians 1:3–4: "Blessed *be* the God and Father of our Lord Jesus Christ, the Father of mercies and God of all comfort, who comforts us in all our affliction so that we will be able to comfort those who are in any affliction with the comfort with which we ourselves are comforted by God." It was obvious that God was using not only my degree from the seminary, but also my master's degree in psychology, my background in pastoral counseling, and my own experiences navigating the chaos of my father's suicide to position me for service in my role as chaplain. It truly was the dream job I had waited for all my life. How many people can say that for thirty years they got to do exactly what God designed them to do? My cup is truly full.

As I have grown older, I have discovered that age brings its own unique stressors with it. As time passed, my health became a source of worry and fear both for myself and for everyone around me. I suffered a series of heart attacks over the course of several years, and I eventually faced quadruple bypass surgery. Following the onset of my heart issues, I also began to suffer from recurring cancer in my bladder that requires constant vigilance to prevent long-term problems. Through many anxious nights in hospital waiting rooms, Shirley—who always seemed immune to any serious health problems—went through the Five Ps as I lay unconscious after surgery. For many years my health has been a source of concern for my family, so it came as a great shock when the roles reversed and it was Shirley who faced a serious problem.

In the midst of all my medical issues, Shirley seemed to be uniquely groomed by God to care for me. She never seemed to face any significant health problems of her own, with one exception. A botched double knee replacement a number of years ago left her mobility compromised. She eventually began using a walker for stability when necessary, but the unsteadiness of her movement was mostly just an inconvenience. Then, in the spring of 2014, Shirley fell and hit her head in our home. Despite her protests, I called an ambulance and we rushed to the hospital. After various tests and scans, the doctors declared that she had nothing more than a bump on the head. The doctors told us that she would undoubtedly have a colorful, prize-winning bruise, but they assured us that everything was okay.

How wrong they were.

About a month later, Shirley began to be lethargic and hesitant to speak. Over the course of only a few days, her condition deteriorated until she was barely responsive to any stimulation. On Father's Day of 2014, we took her to the emergency room, where she was admitted to the hospital under the care of a neurosurgeon. New scans indicated that the previous fall had been far more serious than originally suspected. She had two large pools of blood (subdural hematomas) creating severe pressure on her brain. The neurologist recommended surgery, but he wanted to wait a week to allow certain conditions to become more favorable for the procedure. But her condition continued to worsen. She slept most of the time, and when she was awake she was disoriented and unable to speak coherently. Within three days she was slipping in and out of a coma. The neurosurgeon performed emergency surgery that very day.

I cried out to God. This wasn't how things were supposed to happen. I was the one who had suffered all the health issues. Shirley was my rock and the one person who was able to care for me. While no one spoke openly about it, we all just assumed that God's plan had always been for me to die and go home before Shirley. After all, how could I possibly become a caregiver to the woman who had always been caregiver to me? And if she didn't survive the procedure—what would I do? It was so difficult to sit and await the results of the surgery. What would the doctor say?

When at last the doctor emerged, his news was generally good. They had drained the blood and therefore relieved the pressure on the brain. In theory this should allow the brain the opportunity to work properly again, but there were no guarantees about how much progress we could expect. It was all a matter of time. He encouraged us to remember that progress would likely be very slow; we would need a year to see how far her recovery would go. It was such a relief to hear my sweetheart's voice when she awoke from her anesthesia. She was by no means out of the woods, but it was obvious even in those first moments that the surgery had already improved her condition. We offered joyful prayers of thanksgiving for God's deliverance through this ordeal. Nonetheless, I was about to find out that this trial was far from over.

Over the next few months, Shirley began to stair-step down the various levels of hospital care—ICU, regular room, rehab facility—until she was finally released to go home. During that time I was trying to juggle the commitments of my job and the needs of my precious wife. It seemed like a million decisions were thrown at me every day, and I hardly felt qualified to make any of them. Were it not for the help of my children, I would have sunk. However, it became obvious that I would need to retire from my job and stay at home if I was going to care properly for Shirley. This wasn't easy for me, but not because I lack love for my wife. She is without a doubt the most important person in the world to me. However, I loved my job—my ministry—as the chaplain at DTS. And while I had known for the past couple of years that my time of retirement wasn't far off, I never imagined it happening under these circumstances. I'm a planner by nature, and this was definitely *not* the way I had planned to end my career. I also discovered that caring for someone—even someone you love above all others—is complex and difficult work. I often felt overwhelmed and completely out of my depth when it came to taking care of Shirley, and this was exacerbated by the fact that she was still re-learning how to express herself with words. Suffice it to say that frustration and anxiety were waiting at the foot of the bed every morning when we woke up. By all accounts this new life of mine ought to be a dream. After all, who wouldn't want to retire and spend his days with the love of his life? And while it was certainly true that these basic realities were wonderful, each day still brought a fresh delivery of unexpected challenges to both Shirley and me. The Five Ps took on an even greater depth of meaning as we faced each day in this new life of ours.

While Shirley was still in rehab, the doctors around us began using a phrase that has taken on great significance for us: "new normal." They often told us things like, "You're just going to have to find your 'new normal' as you adjust to having Shirley home." The implication was always that things could not remain the way they had been. Yet they didn't say, "Get used to your new limitations," or, "The life you once had is now over." No, they all simply referred to a new normal; it was neither positive nor negative. As I look at life now, I see that they were right. Did we lose some of the freedom we had before Shirley's fall? Yes. Do we savor every moment now that we recognize how close we came to losing her? You bet. Do I miss my ministry to students now that I'm no longer chaplain at a seminary? Yes. Do I relish my new ministry to my soul mate? Absolutely. Are there difficulties associated with this new normal? Yes. Did we also face unique difficulties before all this happened? Of course. Even in the midst of creating our new normal, God has allowed Shirley and me to gain some perspective as we look at life through a lens containing almost eighty years. Here is a list of maxims I found written in Shirley's own handwriting:

- We should care more for holiness than hygiene.
- We should be more concerned with how we live than how we look.
- We should spend more time working on our hearts than our hair.
- We should have more praise parties than pity parties.
- We should do more serving than shopping.
- We should be more focused on comforting than on being comforted.

As I look at this list I am thankful not only for the truth it reveals, but for the very fact that my darling wife can still think and write!

Make no mistake: life is much more than any one struggle. Again Larry Crabb offers keen insight: "Healthy people deeply enjoy God, expressed with occasional bursts of ecstasy followed by long periods of quiet allegiance." In many ways, the Five Ps is all about creating a new normal in dealing with any and all adversity in life. Which was better: carrying the burden of being the son of a suicide or the new normal of surrender to God's peace? Perhaps it isn't so strange that we so easily succumb to anxiety. After all, it gives us something to do and a sense of control. "Maybe if I worry enough about this," we think, "I can figure out how to solve it on my own." The Five Ps require us to step away from control and release our burdens—and ourselves—into God's care. Surely that's a new normal worthy of the change.

Discussion Questions

1. In what ways can the concept of the "new normal" be applied in the life of a Christian during both difficulties and times of peace? Are there passages of Scripture that suggest that believers should expect a life of "new normal"?
2. Music was something uniquely therapeutic (but not specifically biblical) that God used in our lives. What thing(s) might God use in someone else's life to help in times of difficulty? What about in your life?
3. The writer offers four steps for constructing a planned biblical response like the Five Ps. Can you identify an area of struggle in your own life that could benefit from having a planned biblical response? How might you begin to construct that response?
4. Who are some people in your own life who can support you as agents of God's change? What can you do to enlist their help in your planned biblical response?

Resources for Further Study

Books

Candy Neely Arrington, *Aftershock: Help, Hope, and Healing in the Wake of Suicide* (Nashville: B & H Publishing, 2003).
Larry Crabb, *Understanding People: Why We Long for Relationship* (Grand Rapids: Zondervan, 1987).
Albert Y. Hsu, *Grieving a Suicide: A Loved One's Search for Comfort, Answers, and Hope* (Downers Grove, IL: InterVarsity Press, 2002).

Songs

"What a Friend We Have in Jesus," lyrics by Joseph M. Scriven.
"Two Sparrows in a Hurricane," lyrics and music by Mark Alan Springer, performed by Tanya Tucker.

Contributors

THE AUTHORS

Bill Bryan, now retired, taught biblical counseling in his role as associate professor of pastoral ministries at Dallas Theological Seminary. For more than thirty years, he also served as chaplain at DTS, which involved mentoring students, planning chapel programs, leading worship, assisting in seminary conferences, and counseling both students and faculty. Dr. Bryan has ministered for over fifty years in a variety of pastoral areas, including roles as senior and associate pastor, youth minister, and director of music and education.

Steve Calvert is assistant chief of Chaplaincy Services, which provides emotional and spiritual support to emergency responders, their families, and members of our community who have been impacted by crisis and/or tragedy. He is also the founder of Performance Consultant: NewLife Skills Coaching and Consulting, an organization that provides dynamic personal and organizational coaching and training in all areas of human resources development.

Mary Klentzman is the executive director of Cornerstone Ranch, a Christian home and day program for adults with disabilities. She is a contributor for *Exceptional Teaching: A Comprehensive Guide for Including Students with Disabilities.* She serves on the several Texas state-wide councils through which she has opportunities to influence legislation and state policy impacting children, youth, and adults with disabilities. Mary and her husband, Rick, live in Plano, Texas, and have seven children, including an adult who has multiple disabilities.

Mark McGinniss is associate professor of Old Testament at Baptist Bible Seminary in Clarks Summit, PA. His special interest is the Song of Songs. Mark and his wife, Joy, have five grown children; four daughters-in-laws; one son-in-law; two grandchildren, and zero pets.

Rick Rood has served as a pastor, seminary instructor, and since 1996 has served as chaplain at both an acute care and a psychiatric hospital in the Dallas area. He cared for his wife, Polly, until her home going in 2003. They have a son and daughter. He and his new wife, Li Lin, were married in Taipei, Taiwan, in 2012. They reside in the Dallas area.

Joni Eareckson Tada is the founder and CEO of Joni and Friends International Disability Center, an international advocate for people with disabilities. A diving accident in 1967 left Joni, then 17, a quadriplegic in a wheelchair. After two years of rehabilitation, she emerged with new skill and a fresh determination to help others in similar situations. She founded Joni and Friends in 1979 to provide Christ-centered programs to special-needs families, as well as training to churches. Joni's lifelong passion is to bring the gospel to the world's one billion people with disabilities. Joni survived stage-3 breast cancer in 2010, yet keeps a very active ministry schedule. She and her husband Ken were married in 1982 and reside in Calabasas, California. You can learn more about Joni's ministry at http://www.joniandfriends .org or can write her at response@joniandfriends.org.

Mark R. Talbot is associate professor of philosophy at Wheaton College, Wheaton, Illinois. Prior to coming to Wheaton, he taught at Calvin College in Grand Rapids, Michigan. Before that he was an Andrew Mellon Graduate Fellow at the University of Pennsylvania, where he earned his Ph.D. in philosophy with a dissertation on David Hume's epistemology and won the Dean's Award for Distinguished Teaching by a Graduate Student in the School of Arts and Sciences. Among his publications are *Limning the Psyche: Explorations in Christian Psychology*, which he edited with Robert C. Roberts; *The Signs of True Conversion*; *Should We Leave Our Churches? A Biblical Response to Harold Camping*, with J. Ligon Duncan); and *Personal Identity in Theological Perspective*, which he edited with Richard Lints and Michael Horton. He is married to Cindy and has one married daughter and three grandchildren.

Larry J. Waters is professor of Bible exposition at Dallas Theological Seminary and the lead editor of its academic journal, *Bibliotheca Sacra*. He is the author and editor of several books, including *Why, O God?*, *The Contribution of the Speeches of Elihu to the Argument about Suffering in the Book of Job*, and *A Commentary on the Book of Job*. He is a contributor to *Connecting for Christ: Overcoming Challenges across Cultures* and *Beyond Suffering: A Christian View on Disability Ministry* Larry and his wife, Mary, served as missionaries in the Philippines from 1973 to 1999.

Wayne Walker is a pastor to the homeless and executive director of *OurCalling, Inc.*, which strives to see believers involved in God's work by bridging the gap between the homeless and the housed community

THE ARTIST

Deanna Jones has been a member and facilitator for the New Jersey Writing Project in Texas, Dallas Poets Community, and the Los Angeles Poets and Writers Collective. In addition, she has had work showcased in the Visual Arts Guild of Frisco, Texas Visual Arts Association, Parks Cities Presbyterian Arts Festival, and Faith Artists. Her essays and poetry have been published in *Sulphur River Literary Review, Descant, Rattle,* and *The Yale Book Project* among others. Her photography has been published in *JPG Magazine, Frisco Style,* and *23 on 23: Explorations on the 23rd Psalm* by Park Cities Presbyterian. A daughter of missionaries, she graduated from Dallas Baptist University. Her website is www.cocoriahphoto.com.